Scorpio

Scorpio

OCTOBER 24–NOVEMBER 22

Your Sun-and-Moon Guide
to Love and Life

Ronnie Dreyer

Ariel Books

**Andrews McMeel
Publishing**

Kansas City

www.andrewsmcmeel.com

Interior artwork by Robyn Officer

ISBN: 0-8362-3565-7

Library of Congress Catalog Card Number: 97-71536

Contents

Contents

Contents

Contents

Scorpio

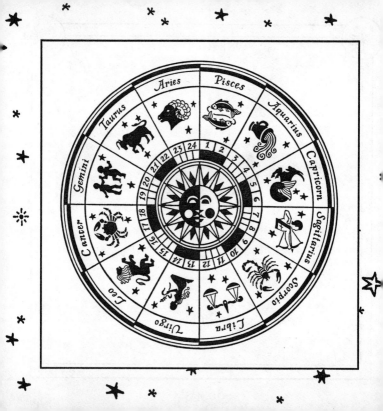

Introduction

Low, *you ask, might*
astrology make a difference in your life,
in your mental, emotional, and spiritual

growth? Of course, there is no single answer to this question, for the responses are as diverse as humanity itself. Some of us may wish to dabble, enjoying astrology as we would a new hobby; have some fun; check out our sign and the signs of our friends, lovers, and children; and muse over the romantic possibilities of various combinations. What, for example, are the chances that a Libra man and a Pisces woman would hit it off? Others of us might wish to embark on a lifelong adventure, plumbing the depths of esoteric wisdom and emerging with startling new revelations about ourselves and our lives. Whatever your interest, you will find that astrology has something for everyone.

Astrology, which began as a search for a pattern in the cosmos, is based on the relationship between the infinitely large and the infinitely small, between the macrocosm—primarily our solar system, with its Sun, Moon, and planets, but also the fixed stars beyond—and the microcosm, the mysterious individual personality. In other words, astrology is the study of how celestial bodies influence the Earth and affect the human beings who dwell here.

In this regard, it's important to understand that astrology deals with symbols. The signs of the zodiac represent

14

powerful forces, profound energies of the mind, heart, and soul. These energies are expressed in our personal horoscope, or birth chart, which describes the position of the heavens at our moment of birth and therefore portrays our unique personalities, our likes and dislikes, our strengths and weaknesses, our hopes and fears.

A horoscope is not, however, a simple reading of the future, a trip to the fortune-teller. You might want to consider your horoscope as a kind of map, indicating, say, the model of car you are driving, the condition of its motor, the state of the road (which may be bumpy in some places and smooth in others), and the variety of spiritual and emotional terrain you are likely to encounter during your life's journey. Perhaps the motor needs a tune-up; perhaps two roads pass through a particular stretch of wilderness, one road potholed and poor, the other sure and clear; perhaps just off the beaten path lies a great marvel you would miss if you didn't know it was there. What you do with the map astrology provides is up to you: You are free to choose, free to act as you will, free to make the most of your life—and, too, free to have plenty of fun along the way.

A Brief
History

Long ago, men and women looked up into the starry night sky and wondered what it was and what effect it had on their lives. From that first primordial inquiry, astrology was born. No one quite knows how far back astrology's oral tradition extends; its first appearance in recorded history dates to 2500 B.C. in ancient Mesopotamia, where it was believed that the heavenly bodies were great gods with powers to influence the course of human affairs. Those early astrologers began to observe the heavens carefully and keep systematic records of what they saw in the great glittering silence of the night sky. The royal family's astrological counselors advised them on how to rule; early in its history, astrology was considered the "royal art."

The ancient Greeks already boasted

an ample pantheon of gods by the time their astronomers began to use the new science of geometry to explain the workings of the heavens. The Greeks combined Mesopotamia's form of astrological divination with their own mythology and the new science of geometry, developing a personal astrology based on the zodiac—from the Greek *zodiakos kyklos*, or "circle of animals"—a belt extending nine degrees on either side of the ecliptic, the Sun's apparent annual path across the sky. The belt was divided into segments named after animals—the Ram, the Bull, the Crab—and set to correspond to certain dates of the year. The Greeks were thus able to use astrology to counsel individuals who were curious about the effect of the heavens on their lives; the art of reading personal horoscopes was born.

As one seer of the times said, speaking of the heavens, "There is no speech nor language where their voice is not heard." Astrology was incorporated into Roman culture and spread with the extension of the Roman Empire throughout Europe. With the rise of Christianity, astrology faced a challenge: After all, it seemed to suggest that humans were determined by the stars, rather than by the stars' creator, who also, according to emerging Christian theology, had granted humans free will. Generally, however, astrology was absorbed into Christian teachings and continued to flourish; witness the selection of an astrological date for Christmas. Like much of classical culture, astrology went into decline during the Middle Ages, emerging in the early Renaissance to occupy a privileged place in the world of learning; in the sixteenth and seventeenth centuries, it was embraced by the prominent astronomers

Tycho Brahe and Johannes Kepler and was taught as a science in Europe's great universities.

Eventually, the discoveries of modern science began to erode the widely held belief in astrology's absolute scientific veracity. In our times, though, astrology remains as popular as ever, as an alternative to scientific theory, and as a way for people to articulate the manifold richness of the self. Psychologist Carl

Jung noted that astrology "contains all the wisdom of antiquity"; for modern men and women in search of the soul, it holds perennial interest as an expression of the psyche's mysterious relationship to the myriad wonders of the universe.

The Heavens

An Overview

In astrology, the art of relating events on Earth to influences in the heavens, each celestial body exerts its own form of power, which is modified according to its geometric relationship with the others. The heavens are made up of several kinds of celestial bodies. First, of course, there is the solar system—the Sun, Moon, and planets. Beyond the solar system lies the infinity of fixed stars, so-called because, as opposed to the planets, which the ancients could observe moving across the sky, the stars were always in the same place. Your horoscope plots the placement of the celestial bodies at the time of your birth.

When we speak of the heavens in astrology, we often speak of the zodiac, an imaginary belt extending nine degrees on either side of the ecliptic, the apparent path of the Sun across the sky. (Remember that the zodiac was devised in antiquity, when it was believed that the Sun revolved around the Earth.) The zodiac is divided into twelve arcs, or constellations, of thirty degrees each. Each arc is accorded a name and associated with the dates during which the Sun made its annual passage through that region of the sky at the time the zodiac was first devised. Your sun sign, the most widely known of the many astrological signs, refers to the particular arc of the zodiac through which the Sun was passing at the time of your birth. (With the procession of the equinoxes, the solar path may not always correspond to the actual solar chart.) The zodiac belt also contains the orbits of the Moon and most of the planets.

The solar system, then, constitutes the most important influence on human affairs. In ancient times, it was believed that the planets had their own light (the Sun and Moon were considered planets). Only five planets—Mercury, Venus, Mars, Jupiter, and Saturn—were visible to the ancients; Uranus, Neptune, and Pluto have been discovered over the last two hundred years. The influence of each planet depends on its position in the zodiac and its relation to the other celestial bodies, including the fixed stars. While some astrologers maintain that the planets are primarily refractors of influences from the more distant stars, most believe that each planet, along with the Sun and Moon, has its own characteristics that uniquely influence us—how we think, feel, and act. This influence can be positive and constructive or negative and self-destructive. Ultimately, the planets' disposition in your chart is a way of expressing various possibilities, which you can interpret and act upon as you choose.

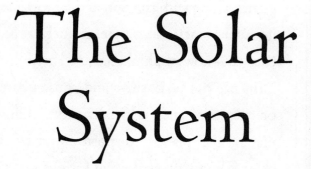

The Solar
System

M ost astrologers
agree that the primary

influences come from within our own solar system—the Sun, Moon, and planets. Each planet is said to rule over one or two signs of the zodiac and have sway over a particular part of the body. Over the centuries, each planet has come to represent or influence a different aspect of the personality.

The Sun, which rules Leo, represents the conscious, creative aspects of the self. In a chart, a well-placed, strong

Sun indicates a dignified, self-possessed, affectionate, and authoritative personality; a badly placed Sun can suggest an ostentatious and dictatorial nature. The Sun rules the heart. Solar types tend to be energetic (the Sun, after all, is our source of energy) and like to take on large-scale projects that make good use of their many talents. They often make excellent top-level executives.

On the other hand, the Moon,

which rules over zodiacal Cancer, represents the imagination and is often linked by astrologers with the unconscious, hidden part of humans. In a chart, a prominent Moon usually indicates a sensitive and vulnerable nature, which can often be quite delightful; a badly placed Moon, however, can suggest an unhealthy and even dangerous self-absorption. In terms of the body, the Moon rules over the breasts. Lunarians are adaptable and often protective; perfectly capable of enjoying the delights of a quiet life at home, many also seek the public spotlight.

Mercury, the smallest planet and the one closest to the Sun, rules Gemini and Virgo. Like the Roman messenger of the gods whose name it shares, Mercury represents communication, speech, and wit, along with an often changeable disposition. Mercurians tend to be sensitive to their environment; they epitomize verbal and written expression and are often journalists and writers.

Venus, the most brilliant planet, rules Taurus and Libra; the planet of love, it governs the higher emotions, physical beauty, creativity, sex appeal, and sensual experience in all its many forms. It has rule over the throat. Venusians love beauty and art; they can at times be concerned with the surface of things, allowing image to become everything.

Mars, the planet that physically most resembles Earth, rules over Aries; representing the physical side of life, it combines with Venus to influence our sex drive. In a chart, Mars means courage, confidence, and the aggressive urges— the result-oriented ability to take on a project and get it done. In terms of the body, Mars has sway over the sex organs, particularly for men.

Jupiter, the largest planet in the solar

system, rules Sagittarius and represents the more profound realms of thinking and mental life, as well as the depths of the spirit. Jupiter suggests generosity, loyalty, success, and steady, solid growth. In terms of the body, it has sway over the thighs, liver, and blood. Jupiterians tend to be thoughtful, even philosophical, with plenty of social skills and an adventurous love of travel; Jupiter women are often strikingly beautiful.

Saturn, the farthest from Earth of the traditional planets, represents fears, uncertainties, and materialistic concerns. It can indicate practicality, patience, and honesty, although, if badly placed in a chart, Saturn can also suggest a deep fear of life. It governs the human skeleton, emphasizing this planet's role in providing structure and control; Saturnians tend to make good accountants and bureaucrats.

Uranus, discovered in the eighteenth century, rules Aquarius. Often representing change, even upheaval, it can be a beneficent influence, representing the kind of brilliant flash of insight that can instigate bold new ways of thinking. Yet its independent and rebellious nature can pose problems, when liberty turns to license and at times even to crime.

Neptune, discovered in the mid-nineteenth century, has rule over Pisces.

On its beneficent side, it can represent idealism, art, and imagination; its connection with the sea (Neptune was the Roman god of the ocean) indicates its tendency to affect the unconscious aspects of the psyche. This can bring great power; it can also, however, suggest a preference to dream rather than act.

Pluto, discovered in 1930, now rules Scorpio. The planet farthest from the Sun, Pluto often represents the dark forces of desire and instinct that seek dissolution of the self within the great cosmos. While there are dangers here, there is as well the potential for profound healing.

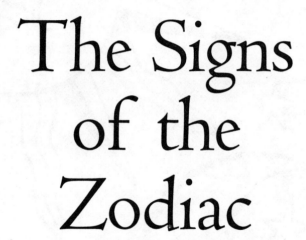

The Signs of the Zodiac

When we speak
of the signs of the zodiac,

we refer to the twelve thirty-degree arcs of the sky into which the zodiac is divided. Each sign is represented by an image derived from ancient descriptions of the constellations; however, the astrological signs of the zodiac should not be confused with the actual constellations whose names they sometimes share. The most important signs are the sun signs, by which is meant the particular zone of the sky through which the Sun was passing at the time of someone's birth.

The signs of the zodiac are as follows:

Aries (the Ram), March 21–April 20

Taurus (the Bull), April 21–May 21

Gemini (the Twins), May 22–June 21

Cancer (the Crab), June 22–July 23

Leo (the Lion), July 24–August 23

Virgo (the Virgin), August 24–September 23

Libra (the Scales), September 24–October 23

Scorpio (the Scorpion), October 24–November 22

Sagittarius (the Archer), November 23–December 21

Capricorn (the Goat), December 22–January 20

Aquarius (the Water Bearer), January 21–February 19

Pisces (the Fish), February 20–March 20

The zodiacal signs are also symbols for the great forces that lie deeply within our minds, hearts, and souls and exist in different combinations from one person to the next. Each sign is associated with a different part of the body. In total, the twelve signs express all that we are as humans. The signs are said to be composed of four different elements and three different qualities.

The Four Elements

The *four elements* through which the twelve signs of the zodiac are expressed are fire, earth, air, and water. For the Greeks, they were the fundamental substances of the universe. In astrology, these elements are also spiritual and symbolic; they are expressed in connection with three different qualities—cardinal, fixed, and mutable. Each element has one cardinal sign, one fixed sign, and one mutable sign; and each quality is expressed through each element, as in the chart that follows:

	Cardinal	*Fixed*	*Mutable*
Fire	Aries	Leo	Sagittarius
Earth	Capricorn	Taurus	Virgo
Air	Libra	Aquarius	Gemini
Water	Cancer	Scorpio	Pisces

In addition, the four elements, which are restless and in conflict with one another, are often said to be bound together by a mysterious, invisible fifth element, known as the "quintessence," which is responsible for maintaining the often tenuous unity of all things on Earth.

Fire Signs

The fire element, expressed through Aries, Leo, and Sagittarius, is profoundly linked to the spirit. Fire is a powerful elemental force; impulsive, iconoclastic, and warm, the fire signs are eternally seeking expression. If not regulated in some way, however, fire can turn destructive, burning out of control.

Aries—outgoing, idealistic, enthusiastic—requires great freedom in order to achieve its maximum sense of self. Often brimming with confidence, the Aries type tends to act impulsively and not always with proper concern for what other people may think or feel. This spontaneity can be tremendously attractive, but it can at times become selfish and overbearing.

Leo, on the other hand, while also possessing a deep need for freedom, tends to be much more sensitive to others. Given to the exuberant and flamboyant, Leo's creativity is frequently expressed through art and drama. Self-reliant and generally optimistic, the Leo nature also has a vein of altruism; Leos can, though, at times be a bit vain.

Sagittarius, the mutable fire sign, is characterized by qualities of profound yearning and aspiration. Open, honest, and generous, Sagittarians tend to be hungry for growth and expansion. They are very independent—sometimes to a fault—and are often great seekers, for whom the journey is more important than the destination.

Earth Signs

*T*he earth element, expressed through Taurus, Virgo, and Capricorn, is deeply connected to physical things. Generally, it reflects the practical, down-to-earth side of human nature. It is also said to be an incarnating principle by which spirituality takes on form. Not surprisingly, the earth and water elements enjoy a close relationship, with earth stabilizing water and water making the arid earth fertile.

Taurus, the fixed earth sign, tends toward the sedentary. Slow, practical, and conservative, a person born under Taurus will likely evidence an unspectacular, solid determination. Taurus is receptive to the joys of a gentle, stable existence—a regular paycheck, a nice house, warm relationships, a comfortable routine. When frustrated or threatened, however, the Taurus nature can turn possessive and jealous.

Virgo, the mutable earth element, is drawn toward ephemeral things, engrossed in "what is past, or passing, or to come." Intellectual, elegant, intelligent, and methodical, Virgo is driven to seek the clarity of understanding. When subjected to intense stress, though, Virgo can become hypercritical and a bit of a nag.

Capricorn, the cardinal earth element, is dependable, solid, trustworthy, and prudent. The Capricorn nature will plow steadily ahead, connected to its roots and clear about what it wishes to achieve in life. Yet in stressful situations Capricorn can become selfish and rigid.

Air Signs

The air element, expressed
through Gemini, Libra, and Aquarius,
has long been associated with thought,
dating back to the ancient concept that

thinking is the process by which humans take in ideas from the world around them, much as they take in air through breathing. All three air signs generally are dominated by tendencies toward restlessness; they are also known as the nervous signs. However, they are each unique.

Gemini is particularly volatile, a whirlwind constantly blowing in many directions. The Gemini nature is inventive, alert, and communicative, but Geminis can at times become unstable and wild, even hysterical.

Libra is like a strong wind that blows purposefully in a single direction. Its influence is elegant and orderly. Libras tend to be perceptive and affectionate, sensitive to others and aware of their needs, although in excess a Libra nature can be impractical and a bit lazy.

Aquarius, the calmest air sign, is associated with water as well as air; it represents spiritual knowledge, creativity, and freedom. The Aquarian nature tends toward the rational and places great value on freedom, sometimes sacrificing the future in the name of rebellion.

Water Signs

*T*he water element, expressed through Cancer, Pisces, and Scorpio, represents the fluidity, spirituality, and sensitivity in our nature. Often emotional, sometimes to the point of instability, the water element needs to find some kind of container in order to realize its true potential.

Cancer, represented by the Crab, is emotional, imaginative, and romantic; it can also be very cautious. There is something gentle and shy about the Cancer nature; afraid of being hurt, it is sometimes slow to come out of—and quick to return to—its shell. Such vulnerability can be deeply touching; in excess, however, it can turn moody and self-absorbed.

Scorpio, the most self-confident of the water signs, is masterful, shrewd, and determined. Possessed of strong desires, Scorpio types are not easily dissuaded from pursuing their goals. In doing so, they can be forceful and inspirational; yet when threatened, they can exhibit a violent streak, and when thwarted they can turn sarcastic and cruel.

Emotional and highly intuitive Pisces is also quick to retreat from the slings and arrows of life. Often this is because the Pisces nature is so sensitive to the emotional needs of others that it will sometimes forget its own interests and need to seek temporary refuge, in order to find its own center again. It has to be careful, though, not to fall into the trap of self-pity.

The Three Qualities

There are three quali-ties, or modes of expression, through which each of the four elements finds expression in the twelve signs of the zodiac: cardinality, fixity, and mutability.

The qualities are another way of expressing features the different signs share; all four fixed signs, for example, will have certain features in common, in that they will tend to be more stable than the mutable signs within their same element. This may seem complicated, but the basic principle is actually pretty simple.

The cardinal quality serves as the origin of action, the wellspring of energy that gets things done in the world. It's the "mover and shaker" personality—active, outward-looking, more geared to "do-ing" than to "being." The four cardinal signs are Aries, Cancer, Libra, and Capricorn; each is self-assertive, but in a unique way. Capricorn, the earth cardinal sign, tends to take solid, dependable action that is often geared toward material success, while Aries, the fire sign, often acts in a much more spontaneous, even impulsive, way. Libra, the air sign, is particularly assertive on the intellectual level, quick to advance its ideas and defend them when they are questioned. Cancer, the water sign, tends toward caution and often will act prudently.

The fixed quality serves to temper movement; it functions as an impediment, an often valuable check on the rampant free flow of energy. Sometimes expressed as "will," the fixed signs—Taurus, Leo, Scorpio, and Aquarius—are likely to be resistant to change and appreciate tradition and known, sure values. Taurus, the earth sign, is the most sedentary of all, with deep, latent powers and a clear preference for staying in one place. Leo, the fire sign, embodies a sustained emotional warmth and loyalty that is not likely to change over time. With Scorpio, the water sign, power takes on a more fluid form, exhibiting an unshakable self-confidence that remains firm in the face of adversity. Aquarius, meanwhile, is the most cool and composed of the air signs; Aquarians trust rational thinking and extend deep roots into the ideas they hold and the places where they live.

The mutable quality embodies the principles of flexibility and adaptability. The mutable signs—Gemini, Virgo, Sagittarius, and Pisces—could be said to combine aspects of cardinal impulsiveness with those of the unyielding fixed temperament. Gemini, the mutable air sign, is particularly given to surprising transformations of the self; you think you know a Gemini, and then, *presto!* you realize that you knew only one side of the person's nature. Virgo, the earth sign, is often irresistibly drawn toward the shifting play of ideas and thought. For Sagittarius, the fire sign, change often equals growth; driven to expand, the Sagittarian nature seems eternally questing after something new. Pisces, the water sign, often embodies the fluid, changing character of the emotions; sensitive to the smallest alterations of feelings, it can ride the waves of emotional life like a skilled surfer.

Scorpio

An Introduction

Yours *is the most seri-*

ous, secretive, intense, and introspective sign of the zodiac; and like the desert arachnid that supplies your symbol, you are bristling, wary, and ready to take offense at a moment's notice. Your legendary stinger has been known to kill.

Scorpio is a fixed water sign and the eighth of the zodiac. You are a myriad of contradictions. Sympathy, generosity, and fanatical loyalty mark you; yet you are so emotionally vulnerable that you can over-react (even monstrously overreact) to trifles that other signs would not even notice, and still others would laugh at. You scarcely know how to laugh; and if your feelings are hurt, or you think someone has done you wrong, you can only think of one thing: revenge. No one can give a colder shoulder than you, and

yet you in no way consider yourself intimidating or temperamental! But just
ask your friends: They walk on eggshells
every time they approach you.

Your instincts, passions, and tremendous sensuality can be staunch allies
one day, sworn enemies the next. You
find it very difficult to trust and can take
a great while to believe that anyone's intentions are heartfelt. Once you do so,
however, you will open yourself up with-

out hesitation or reserve and give the (literal) shirt off your back. Your high standards and unrealistic expectations do not make it easy for those you love.

The Scorpio glyph seems delicately poised between your two extremes: coiled intensity on the one hand and the release of pent-up aggression on the other.

Myths
and
Legends

World folklore
contains limitless

examples of the hero's journey, from the knight in shining armor rescuing a damsel in distress to the leader of vast armies vanquishing his enemies and defending his homeland. Equally numerous are tales of the naive, would-be hero whose youthful arrogance and impetuosity lead not to glory but to death. Unyielding obstinacy, will, and an imperious sense of indestructibility are classic Scorpio trademarks. They can catapult a mature Scorpion to tremendous success. They can also lead an immature Scorpion to destruction.

The ancient Greco-Roman myth of Phaethon, son of Helios the Sun god, is a telling example of the inability to handle power. Desirous of winning his father's respect, Phaethon pleads with Helios to lend him his horse-drawn chariot for a single day. Helios is against the idea, but Phaeton insists that he is responsible and trustworthy; finally the father gives in, and Phaeton, despite every warning, flies through the constellations and joyously confronts all obstacles thrown in his path. He is ecstatic and overwhelmed by his potent vigor, and for a few brief shining moments, Phaeton believes he rules the heavens.

Then, without warning, a lethal scorpion emerges from its hiding place and threatens the boy with its claws and snapping tail. As soon as he sees it, Phaeton freezes in terror, drops the reins from his nerveless hands, and loses control of the horses. He is too inexperienced to gain his composure and regroup, so the wild horses bolt, run amok, and careen crazily through the sky with Phaeton and the chariot in tow.

The Sun's chariot now veers too near the Earth, setting it ablaze. In order to save the planet from total destruction,

Zeus (or Jupiter), the king of the Greek (or Roman) gods, strikes the chariot with a magical thunderbolt, killing Phaethon and hurling him into the River Eridanus. The daughters of the Sun then mourn the loss of their brother, who ascends to the sky as the planet Venus.

Because Phaethon could not tame the horses, he fails and is inevitably defeated. Similarly, the Scorpio personality must learn to handle its raw energy. The thirst for power may be what drives you to ultimate success, but too often it goes astray, goes to your head, or corrupts. That is when disaster looms.

Symbols
and
Associations

We know rela-
tively little about what

life was like during the age of Scorpio (16,000–14,000 B.C.), except that the Earth was covered with great sheets of ice, and mankind lived largely in caves. Because our knowledge is so scanty, the age of Taurus (4000–2000 B.C.), Scorpio's polar opposite, has to supply clues. This era was dominated by the great desert civilization of Egypt, which was preoccupied with death and reincarnation—themes also associated with your sign.

Every zodiacal sign has a ruling planet and a detrimental planet, which are strengthened and weakened respectively when placed in that particular sign. Each planet is also exalted, at its strongest, or fallen, at its weakest, when placed in a specific sign. Pluto, Roman god of the underworld, rules Scorpio, supplying astonishing power, intensity, and magnetism; but Venus, the planet of love, is detrimental there. Uranus, the planet of independence, is exalted in Scorpio, whereas the changeable and emotional Moon is fallen in that same sign.

Scorpios are *loyal, creative, emotional, passionate, charismatic, sensual, seductive, steady, responsible, workaholic, business-oriented, relentless, enduring, energetic, determined, focused,* and *frugal.*

They are also *destructive, manipulative, jealous, greedy, power-hungry, possessive, vengeful, mean-spirited, controlling, inflexible, narrow-*

minded, ruthless, resentful, stubborn, secretive, and *suspicious.*

Your archetypes are the detective, spy, and explorer. Professions include psychologist, psychiatrist, filmmaker, artist, detective, athlete, actor, deep-sea diver, photographer, researcher, scientist, investment banker, and financier.

Parts of the body ruled by Scorpio include the reproductive organs, genitals, bladder, rectum, and prostate glands.

Pluto governs the endocrine system. Scorpion countries include Norway, Morocco, Syria, and Egypt. Fez, Liverpool, Valencia, New Orleans, and Washington, D.C., are Scorpion cities.

Your color is black. If you were born between October 24 and October 31, your birthstone is opal; if you were born between November 1 and November 22, your birthstone is topaz. Other gems associated with Scorpio are bloodstone, lodestone, malachite, jasper, and vermilion. Scorpio's metal is plutonium.

Plants ruled by Scorpio include bramble, heather, horehound, leek, wormwood, and blackthorn. Flowers are chrysanthemums and lilies. Scorpion foods include onions, watercress, cauliflower, leeks, turnips, radishes, figs, and prunes. Herbs and spices are basil, ginseng, bilberry, garlic, elderberry, chicory, witch hazel, and sage.

Famous Scorpio personalities include Charles Bronson, Richard Burton, Prince Charles, Hillary Clinton, Nadia Comaneci, Charles de Gaulle, Michael Dukakis, Sally Field, Whoopi Goldberg, Princess Grace, Billy Graham, Goldie Hawn, Billie Jean King, Dan Rather, Julia Roberts, Martin Scorsese, Jaclyn Smith, Ted Turner, and Henry Winkler.

Your motto is "Seek and you shall find."

Health
and
Physique

The Scorpio type is
frequently distinguished

by a low forehead, heavy eyebrows, hooked nose, firm mouth, and determined chin. Most commanding, however, are the deep-set and piercing eyes, which seem to bore through everyone you meet. They can even make some people uncomfortable.

Though you may often *appear* cool, calm, and collected, you are frequently under stress. Because you are so very tightly wound and often bottle up your feelings with a vacuum seal, your entire body may be tense. Stiff necks, back pains, hunched shoulders, and bad posture could result. You might try a relaxing massage once a week to relieve aching muscles and joints. This could even prevent an emotional outburst when you feel you can't take another minute of the unbearable pressure you are under.

Every zodiacal sign corresponds to a part of the human anatomy, so the horoscope can reveal which organs and areas of the body may be vulnerable and prone to illness. Your retentive nature and bad eating habits can cause a tendency to bowel disorders, urinary tract infections, hernias, hemorrhoids, bladder infections, and chronic constipation. It may help you to drink eight glasses of water daily and eat fiber-rich foods, which are natural laxatives. Because you tend to take life much too seriously, you may also experience headaches and eyestrain. Make sure you take breaks from your work and go to the window or take occasional walks in order to breathe the fresh air.

The combination of your vivid imagination and melancholic nature could lead to hypochondria, as your tendency to "swallow" your emotions could bring on asthma and respiratory problems. Although you would like to think you can handle everything on your own, you shouldn't hesitate to discuss your feelings with a professional counselor, rather than fall prey to uncontrollable outbursts. Since you like to analyze and tear things apart, you might consider therapy an intellectual exercise rather than a purely therapeutic one.

What you eat can affect how you feel, so cut back on the processed, fatty, sugary foods that you so love and you may experience fewer digestive woes. Various herbal teas may help this sensitive part of your body also. And, of course, there's always exercise to help your body operate at top performance. You will probably find that taking regular walks, going for bike rides, or hopping in the pool for a swim will reduce the stress in your life considerably.

Personality

Legend tells of the scorpion who rode across

a lake on the back of the frog, then stung it to death, and thereby brought about its own demise by drowning. "Why did you do that?" the dying frog inquired. "It is my nature," the drowning scorpion replied.

Obstinate, competitive, ruthless. Potent, dynamic, exciting. Brooding, suspicious, afraid. Loyal, affectionate, hypnotic. You are as changeable and tempestuous as the ocean waves: riding a stupendous crest one moment, plunged into the deepest trenches the next. No emotion or possibility is alien to you, and there is *nothing* you cannot accomplish once you set your mind to achieving your goals; and because you possess incredible intensity and concentration, your mood shifts will take you effortlessly from triumph to tragedy, and back again.

With all your scads of energy begging to be released, you could explode into creative genius. If you do not find a positive outlet for all your desires, you could become a hopeless gambler, overeater, or alcoholic. If you do fall into the abyss, you still possess the courage and determination to claw your way back to the top. If you climb to the top with ease, there's the risk that you might fall off. And although your never-ending quest for artistic perfection can pull you to greatness, it can also lead to dangers at home.

You are an enigma even to those you love. You may overwhelm them with the power of your affections (and mood swings), but if they do not return those affections with the ardency you consider appropriate, you will inevitably be disappointed. And for all of your emotion, dominance, and highly charged sexuality, you may be introverted and fearful when you meet people for the first time. New acquaintances will not find it easy to get to know *you*, because you are so suspicious and constantly on guard.

But, when they do finally crack the ice, a brave new world awaits them. No sign of the zodiac is more difficult or prickly, but no sign of the zodiac soars with greater passion or potential. Once you begin to hypnotize, your friends will always be under your spell; and once you dig your pincers into somebody, you won't let go. Life with you will *never* be dull, and the world's most dizzying roller-coaster ride awaits those who have the courage.

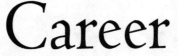

Career

As a child, you may have spent hours

solving complicated jigsaw puzzles or erecting intricate cities out of simple building blocks. That gift for taking things apart and putting them back together again can serve you superbly as a mathematician, chemist, computer programmer, architect, physicist, or engineer. Your fascination with human anatomy and understanding of mysterious states of mind might lead you to be a surgeon, psychiatrist, or research scientist. Your interest in the darker side of life could lead to careers in drug-rehabilitation therapy or bereavement counseling—fields in which you can help others deal with the weaknesses and obsessions you may have wrestled with yourself. Or, on a different tack, your desire for material comfort, intrigue, and risk-taking might attract you to investment banking and financial consulting—for which you have a decided propensity, but which could lead you to

play for very high stakes. Whatever pro-
fession you ultimately choose, you will
become obsessed with reaching the top.

Your greatest challenge will be maintaining the balance between complete autonomy on the one hand, and being part
of a team on the other. Although you are
used to working alone, you would be
wise to have a partner, or even a friend
who can advise you objectively and prevent you from giving up if your vision

does not proceed according to plan. This may prove difficult because you demand the same perfection from others as you do from yourself, but so long as you can work at your own pace and according to your own methods, it will probably be worth a try.

Your remarkable eye and ability to penetrate surfaces, capturing subtle nuances to which others are often oblivious, could make you a wonderful photographer, film director, cinematographer, deep-sea diver, or even detective; and your penchant for unraveling puzzles and solving riddles could lead you to write mystery novels or screenplays, either professionally or as a hobby. As an actor, you could get under the skin of any character you wanted to portray; but, in the end, the vocation you choose is irrelevant. Most important is that you persevere, even under enormous strain, until you finish the job as you see fit, and that you continue to remain an excellent role model and inspiration to those who want to fulfill their innermost dreams.

Love
and
Marriage

*Y*ou have never had problems falling in love,

or luring others into your captivating romantic web, or making your lovers feel there was no one else on Earth. Your magnetic eyes begin to spin the magic, and the rest is mystery: By never quite revealing yourself, by always hoarding a few tantalizing secrets, you will remain an enigma even to those who know and love you most. This is, of course, exactly how you like things to be.

You are secretive by nature, but you

have also studied the psychology of love with some assiduity and carefully culti-vated your techniques in order to protect yourself from disappointment. You hate and fear being alone more than anything else in the world, so you will not hesitate to use any trick in the books to seduce and eventually marry the person of your dreams.

Too often, however, you resort to deceit, led there by your insecurities. No one is more loyal than you are; no one is more afraid that that loyalty will never be returned. When you love, you do so completely and with Vesuvian passion, but always you are tortured by doubt. You will go to almost any lengths to keep your mate by your side, but in so doing you may destroy what you are so very anxious to maintain. When you unleash your possessive tentacles and jealous demons, the world had better beware. If you also unfurl your tail with the poisonous stinger, all will surely be over.

And why? You may have lost in love before, but that does not mean you will, and must, do so again. When your beloved consents to walk down the aisle, that should end your doubts and persecutions. It should also lead to new openness. For too long you have coiled in upon your own secrets and menacingly refused to let anyone pry. Now you have to trust your spouse and trust that you will not get hurt. If you begin to release the daily pressure by talking about what you feel, you will not have to worry about an erupting volcano. Instead, you will be engulfed by a lava flow of affection and love—which you can return with ease. And, as one of the lustiest signs of the zodiac, you'll make sure that the flames of passion between you two never die down.

Home
and
Family

You invite friends over for the evening, and

those visiting for the first time may be surprised at your adamant refusals of help in cleaning up later. Old-timers will only smile, because they know that you insist on being in complete control, whether orchestrating a brilliant party or putting every last paper clip in its proper place. It may sound extreme, and you might even laugh at yourself in retrospect—if you knew how to laugh.

Life is not always a comic masterpiece for those you live with, because your take-charge attitude and obsessive need to have everything your own way can become oppressive after a while. In addition to that, compromise is unlikely: That is unfamiliar territory to you. When your spouse offers to help, you usually refuse because you know that things won't be done as you want. And yet if you do not change your ways—relax, enjoy life more, achieve a little flexibility—your spouse and children might start feeling they live in an armed camp. Is the world going to end if you don't vacuum the rugs once a week? If the kids dread getting fingerprints on your spotless walls, you might as well send them to boarding school. They would probably have more fun there—and less discipline. Your fanaticism is better served, and more useful, at work. Families are supposed to enjoy life together.

Your children will probably be over-achievers; the sad thing is that they will feel they *have* to be. They would be far better off excelling—or even not excelling—because they want to, and not because they need to please you or live up to your exalted and impossible standards. Unhappiness will be the inevitable result. You may think you are setting a perfect example, but in many cases you are only making things more difficult. They can be excellent children who will make you justly proud without in any way being ideal; you must make every effort to praise them when they deserve it—and to applaud more often than you carp. Think about this: Do you really want them to suffer the stress and unhappiness that often marks you? Trying their hardest is much more important than coming in first.

Be a friend rather than a taskmaster,

and your relationship with your children will markedly improve. Set goals by all means, and then let them be free to be children. Remember, childhood should not be boot camp . . . and you do not want a brood of scorpions.

Scorpio
in Love

Though you are noto-rious for being at the mercy of your uncontrollable passions, your idea of romance has less to do with the bedroom than with penetrating the depths of your loved one's psyche and soul. To be sure, you are easily aroused and crave physical contact as much as—perhaps more than—any other sign, but your sexual desires are always tied up with falling in love. For you, sex without love is a way of releasing tension, but nothing more. You desire romance, eros, a profound connection that goes beyond the merely physical. An extended honeymoon on a remote desert island in which you could explore every facet of your love would be paradise, and only an ultimate merging of the body, mind, and soul could satisfy you. Because of this, you can never be

quite sure that you are truly in love, even
if your object of desire seems to be moving Heaven and Earth.

Your emotions are so complex, and
your persona so daunting, that whoever
ventures to take up the gauntlet would almost have to be a paragon of sorts: a
sounding board (or occasionally a dart-
board) for all of your hopes, fears,
doubts, and confusions, as well as an in-
structor who can show you the way out

of your Scorpion darkness. Lovers will come and go, but one day you will find that soul mate to not only brave the black hole of your emotions but to come with you to the end of the tunnel; and this special person deserves all of your respect, fidelity, and devotion.

Scorpio with Aries

MARCH 21–APRIL 20

Y*ou are a roller coaster.*

Aries is a roller coaster of another sort. Will this relationship be as fun as a day at an amusement park? Probably not, though there will ups and downs. This impulsive and aggressive fire sign is a jumble of energy eager to explode, and the Ram requires at least as much physical activity as you do in order to achieve release. Aries, however, simply enjoys being on the move; you need an outlet for all of your boxed-in, tormented emotions.

But each of you has finally found a partner who can keep up with the other's daredevil antics and pace, so whether you want to go scuba diving, mountain climbing, or even bungee jumping, you can do so with a wildly abandoned enthusiast whose heart careens with yours. Despite your many shared energies, however, the two of you differ in significant ways.

Aries is always ready for business or play; it is a sort of perpetual motion machine and never wants to stop. You, too, can be energetic to an extreme; but you can also be torpid, brooding, intensely depressed, and unmoving. Aries lives its life outdoors; when your creative juices are flowing and your mind is busily at work, you can hole up in your office for days on end and never think of leaving except to eat and drink. Aries knows you as the charismatic athlete who flew down that ski slope; you will quickly uncoil the other facets of your complicated, and even demonic, personality. And when the

Ram sees your stinger, it just might bolt.
It will certainly start to fidget.

Yet Aries can also be surprisingly
philosophical, so if you are not ready to
go rafting on a given day—if you are iso-
lated and despondent, or simply busy
with your consuming affairs—the Ram
will gladly take off without you and find
its own way. You are highly independent
in any case, and so is Aries, so that will
be all right with you.

You are also intensely, inordinately jealous, and when the Ram displays too much ease of independence, you may start to fume. Sulking, pouting, and otherwise giving Aries the idea that you want it to wear a bridle will make the Ram bolt for the nearest exit. You are going to have to wrestle with, and conquer, your various furies if you do not want to lose the lovable and joyous Ram. You do command a great many interests that can keep you occupied while Aries is out exploring, so turn to them. Find solace in them or you will be in trouble.

Your emotions are very close to the surface; the Ram often appears not to know what emotions are. Aries does not like to think about feelings, its own or yours, much less discuss them. You love to engage in lengthy chats about your feelings. The Ram, who just wants to get out of the house and get moving, is most likely not the ideal partner for these talks.

Remember that the capering Ram is like a child: For all its independence, it demands attention with an almost simple-minded innocence, and will not be satisfied until you stop whatever you are doing the moment it comes through the door. You, however, will never act on command, and if you are expected to perform, you will probably refuse. On the other hand, you may want to wait just a *little* while before you set Aries straight. Passion comes first, and once you commit yourself to this torrid affair, neither you nor the Ram will ever go away.

Scorpio with Taurus

APRIL 21–MAY 21

You *are focused and* intense; Taurus is lazy and indulgent. You always need something to do with your time; the Bull has an indolent streak a mile long. It can eat, drink, and stare silently into your penetrating eyes for hours on end, or lie on a couch watching TV until the tube blows out. This fixed earth sign loves to sleep late, cuddle lengthily, and take its sweet time before getting out of bed; and once it finally does manage to turn to you for a good-morning kiss, you are already showered, dressed, and ready to sail out the door. You are too fast, and Taurus is too slow;

and these differing styles could lead to loud arguments and endless complaints.

You may even find yourself getting in the car and turning on the ignition to prove that you have every intention of leaving your dawdling mate behind. And then, out of rage and resentment and the seething need to *prove* your point, you may actually do it. Your obstinacy will dig in, and you will not give an inch: As a Scorpio, you are, after all, the second most stubborn sign of the zodiac.

But guess who is first? Taurus is not called the Bull simply because it has horns. Few signs are sweeter or gentler; none is more loving, and none, perhaps, can evince greater patience. Even the Bull, however, has a breaking point; and once you reach it, it will not give so much as a millimeter. Neither of you will compromise—you because you do not know how, and Taurus because you have forced the issue. These clashes can be very dangerous, and you may even have to ask a neutral friend to see you out of your jams. Otherwise, you both may brood until the onset of World War III.

Yet those same passions, when properly channeled, can lead to wonderful harmony and power. Each of you is clinging, and each would like to have the other around constantly. You want the Bull to pay scrupulous attention to your many shifting emotional needs; Taurus wants you to be devoutly passionate and tender. The Bull, who adores the bedroom, would also love to feel your flesh against its own, and you certainly require your nightly release; and this may be the best place for the two of you to work out your many differences and agree on your common wants. You will never slow down, and Taurus will never speed up, but at least you both will fully understand the worth of your desires.

And worth, indeed, can draw you even closer together. Both of you find excitement and creative fulfillment in business proposals, Taurus because it loves to spend money on beautiful things, you because you adore the challenge of the deal. You will have to show patience in order to appreciate the Bull's considerable financial acumen, and Taurus may have to speed up a little to keep pace with your

ingenious plans. Once you have the tim-
ing right, however, the rest of your lives
can fall into place. And passionate lives
they will be.

Scorpio with Gemini

MAY 22–JUNE 21

At first glance, you, so somber and controlled, might seem to have nothing in common with talkative, humorous, and diffuse Gemini, a mutable air sign symbolized by the contradictory Twins—who are always full of ideas but can never make a final decision. You might even want to run from this engagement, given that Gemini can change its mind three or four times in as many minutes, and will try to lure you into the bright and glittering world of people, parties, and nonstop fun—where you are rarely willing to go. But you are also drawn to curiosities and challenges, and the Twins will offer plenty of both. This could be the dare of a lifetime, because myriad are your differences.

You are mysterious and introverted; Gemini is extroverted and open. You like keeping to yourself; Gemini hates to be alone. You take life far too seriously; Gemini takes nothing seriously enough. Gemini's constant chatter and inability to sit still for more than five minutes will drive you crazy; your capacity for stillness and for shutting out the world will make the Twins think they have gone insane. Do you want more?

You are extraordinarily focused and fixated on your goals, and until you have achieved exactly what you desire, you will not even consider starting something new. Gemini has no application or patience: It bores easily, needs to be constantly entertained, and loves juggling at least two or three elements at once. If the

Twins aren't quite satisfied with the job they are doing, they will abandon it midstream without a hesitation or worry and switch to something else. You would be shocked at your failure in such an easy capitulation; the Twins simply take it in stride.

All of these differences, of course, could also light the way to conjunction: You might achieve the perfect tension of opposites that will keep surprise and attraction in a constant state of balance. Gemini's easy charm is hard to resist and could only add luster to your already-numerous allurements. Your passionate intensity fascinates the Twins and could lend depth to their shallow souls. Your relentless focus could give point and direction to Gemini's brilliant, original, but scattershot mind, and Gemini's airy lightness could be just the touch you need to dispel your too-frequent gloom.

The two of you, so remarkably and even diametrically different, could provide wonderful complements to each other's strengths and weaknesses. But you are also so bristlingly independent that you might mutually rebel even against that beneficial interchange.

So perhaps you should concentrate on what splendid business partners you can make. The Twins are brimming with visionary schemes that you can put to practical use; and they can sell anything under the sun. You, in your endless complexity, can find various ways of stimulating their creativity even more, and they can show you how to relax and therefore get a sharper start on *tomorrow's* business, because even you have to unwind some time.

Finally, if both of you are happy and fulfilled, you might even explore the possibilities of the night.

Scorpio with Cancer

*C*ancer is extraordi-narily moody, emotional, and taciturn, sensitive, wary, and complex. It wavers as the water does and can soar into the skies as well as crash into the deeps. When menaced, it will retreat into its shell and threaten never to emerge again, and it may feel threatened all the time because it is as touchy as a hen in a fox's lair. Does any of this sound familiar? Cancer is cardinal, and you are fixed, but both of you are water signs and possibly the most complicated members of the zodiac. Each of you can sympathize to an extraordinary degree, and sense—sometimes *know*—exactly what the other is feeling, and frequently what you feel is paranoia.

When two fanatically secretive and distrustful signs meet, what do they talk about? Scorpio: "They're out to get me." Cancer: "They're out to get all of us, but especially *me*." No one can be trusted, except perhaps yourselves—so now you have found your perfect soul mate. Until one of you turns the other in.

In a lighter (and also more serious)

vein, both of you are ruled by your hearts, which can be magnificent, and not your heads, so you will waste little time analyzing each other's faults. More important still, your extraordinary intuitive understanding will keep you from brooding, lashing out, and turning on the silent treatment, which gives you a tremendous advantage over every other sign. Talking is never easy for either of you, but you two will have less need of it than most. And if you do talk, you will probably be able to stop ugly arguments dead before they are born. If you can't, however, watch out. Armageddon has nothing on a Scorpion and Crab who have taken to their separate cubbyholes to fume and plot revenge.

Both of you are highly emotional and instinctive, but Cancer craves reassurance, whereas you crave only privacy. The Crab is also more sentimental and enjoys a good cry; indeed, its emotions are perhaps a little simpler than yours altogether. Go out of your way to make Cancer feel important and loved, and you will have done much to smooth your remarkable way; and if that entails an occasional evening watching an insufferable tearjerker, so what? Your Crab can provide you a lifetime of genuine feeling in return.

But you will have a delicate balancing act to bring off because you do desperately need to be alone at times, no matter how devotedly you love your mate. Insecure Cancer, however, may easily misunderstand when you tell it to seek out its friends once in a while and give you some time alone. Yet if it heeds you too well and spends too many nights away, you, perversely, may become jealous! Not even a water sign can have it both ways, so you will have to call a

185

truce—or work out your problems in the bedroom.

Two highly suspicious and inarticulate people can communicate instinctually and sensually. You require no protracted conversations in order to satisfy, completely, your needs to love and be loved. Realize that, and you will never be jealous again.

Scorpio with Leo

JULY 24–AUGUST 23

You are brooding, intense, and dark; the Lion is bombastic, benevolent, and bright. You are the fearsome dweller of the desert with the legendary sting; Leo is the resplendent king of the jungle with the legendary roar. That roar is partially bluster and self-enjoying drama, whereas your sting can indeed be deadly. But the Lion is utterly fearless, and when the two of you clash, the heavens will hear your thunder. No two signs of the zodiac are more passionate or enthralling.

Sparks will fly. Well, more than that: Fires will explode. Leo, a fixed fire sign that considers itself a second Sun, demands to be the center of attention wherever it goes: The spotlight is merely an extension of itself. You avoid center stage, but you also crave glory of your own, and you do not want this arrogant feline infringing on your jealously guarded turf. It will: You both may be doing an impossible amount of work, but Leo will take all the credit if given even half a chance—and possibly believe its own falsehoods! And all of it will be great fun.

You are also the two most controlling signs of the zodiac, so battle lines will form early. If you say black, Leo will say white. If you say yes, Leo will say no—on principle. You may not even know what you are fighting about, or what your true feelings are, because you'll be too busy arguing.

If you can stop bickering long

enough, however, you might realize that you share a passionate commitment both to your common ideals and to each other—and that your combined energies could form a new Sun. Alas, although your mutual, constant needs for love and affection may consume your time and seem strong enough to bind you, you remain Dr. Jekyll and Mr. Hyde in too many fundamental matters.

Can the glorious Lion contend with

your dark moods, bouts of depression, and need to be alone? And can you temper your unreasoning jealousy when Leo is surrounded by adoring admirers? The Lion loves to flirt and needs constantly to be petted—but when you go into a black hole and require comfort and support, your busy genius may be creating drama elsewhere. However worshipful its devotion, Leo is also profoundly self-involved. The Lion may be so bursting with its own news that it will scarcely even notice your deep, black, and consuming moods.

So let your Lion know. You always have difficulty expressing your feelings, but Leo is no mind reader, so you had better start quickly, or your rage will fester. And never be afraid to ask for what you need: Leo may be blinded by its own beauty and brilliance, but it is also extraordinarily generous and loving. Mention that you need a little attention, and see how this feline jumps! But watch your tongue: The king of the jungle is very sensitive and proud. Wound it in its ego, and you may destroy its love. Say that it rules the world, on the other hand, and the zodiac may have to invent new superlatives for you both.

Scorpio with Virgo

V*irgo, a mutable earth* sign symbolized by a gentle maiden carrying a sheaf of harvested corn, is maniacally fastidious and analyzes every situation until ashes alone remain. Virgins are the most meticulous members of the zodiac, but you run them a respectable second. No other signs can understand and even identify with so many characteristic idiosyncrasies (which to you and the Virgin seem perfectly natural), and both of you are compulsive to a fault.

Each likes to stay constantly occupied, so neither will think twice about working long into the night; and if you are a perfectionist, then Virgo is a double perfectionist in everything it does. The Virgin will never be satisfied until every tiniest "i" is dotted and every particle of offending lint is removed from the couch. You may nod your head in recognition of the Virgin's behavior, but fundamental differences will haunt you nonetheless.

Though bashful, self-conscious, and

perhaps as introspective as you are, Virgo can nevertheless talk eight to the bar once it feels at ease. You are never at ease with words and would infinitely rather remain silent; and although your appreciative mate may be grateful that you are a superior listener, the Virgin will still try to extract your secrets. This you cannot allow. *No one* can pry into your life without your permission; but Virgo is a good Samaritan, mother hen, and zodiacal social worker rolled into one, and the Virgin is always confident that it knows what is best for you. To you, an intrusion is still an intrusion, no matter how good Virgo's intentions are. If the Virgin asks you even one question that you don't feel like answering, you may find yourself a very grumpy Scorpion.

You had better warn your mate at the outset that you will reveal yourself in your own time, and that the more the

Virgin pries, the colder you are likely to grow. Worse still, you might be forced to unleash your venomous sting—and both of you could regret that for the rest of your lives. Virgo, in the end, is very meek and humble, and the ugliness of your temper could conceivably drive this sign away for good.

Before that dire event, therefore, tell the Virgin firmly but gently that you will come around in time. Virgo gives freely—it is a very generous sign—but you take far longer to dole out your trust. Once you do so, however, you will never let go—and your loyalty is legend. So, of course, is your temper, so you must warn the Virgin not to take your moods personally. If Virgo can play the role of caregiver to your sufferer-in-need, then all should be well; and although you generally shun assistance, and bristle at the very idea that you need it, you should be willing to make an exception for this exceptionally gentle sign.

And then? The Virgin loves to keep in shape, and your moods are tempered by physical release, so perhaps you could work out together, build up a sweat, and then cool down at home in your own private sanctuary. The shower is close at hand, and you should enjoy it together.

Scorpio with Libra

SEPTEMBER 24–OCTOBER 23

When loving, artistic, and marriage-minded Libra strolls into your life, you will have difficulty saying no. This cardinal air sign is one of the most romantic and persuasive members of the zodiac; and when Libra wants something, it usually gets it. And Libra always knows what it wants. At the same time, however, Libra is consumed by the pursuit of harmony and fairness. Its very symbol, indeed, is the balancing Scales of Justice. How can such a paragon be attracted to you?

You, after all, are a prickly soul and a troublemaker in many ways, and you will never think twice about stirring up a fight. You like to play devil's advocate; you like to burst bubbles. Libra, because it is so judiciously fair-minded, can see every side of an issue, but it will never argue one or another simply to cause dissension. Intellectually you are far apart.

Emotionally, as well, you may have trouble because the Scales are airy and light, whereas you are obsessive and heavy. You want to penetrate only one person's soul, but do it to the absolute bottom. The Scales, without fanaticism, need to be adored, however triflingly, by everyone they meet; and although they may love only you, they need to flirt with the rest of the world. Libra is the great networker of the zodiac, unfulfilled unless it has had fifty conversations a day with forty-five different people. You are the great recluse who wants only to retreat from the crowd. You would seem to have nothing in common, and yet the two of you, despite all of your formidable differences, love being together; and friends may be baffled at the sight.

Why? Libra requires attention, and no sign is more concentrated or attentive than you—so long as you choose to have nothing else on your mind. The Scales also envy the intensity you bring to every aspect of your life, which contrasts so strikingly with their own lightness. You, in turn, admire Libra's elegance and ease, its delicacy of touch, the confidence, exactitude, and sheer charming beauty it brings to human relations. The Scales can also lift you effortlessly out of even your blackest moods, which to you is akin to magic; and that indeed is Libra's specialty: balance, diplomacy, understanding, keeping people together and happy, and making them feel on top of the world. The Scales are, in fact, the great manipulators of the zodiac . . . but always gentle, affectionate, and actuated by the most generous and selfless motives.

You, therefore, must understand that Libra's socializing and innocent flirtation, which are so alien to your somber nature, are part and parcel of its magic. The Scales will remain loyal and true, and at 5 P.M. they are yours alone. You cannot distinguish between work and play; Libra can do so with its eyes closed.

Let the Scales teach you a little about balance and the art of compromise, and learn, perhaps, a little more about staying home every now and then. Assure Libra of your understanding and love, and you will discover all the grace that lies in harmony.

Scorpio with Scorpio

OCTOBER 24–NOVEMBER 22

Brooding, *intense, pas-*
sionate, manipulative, torrential, and
possibly venomous—when Scorpion
meets Scorpion, even the thunder will

run and hide. This will either be the most exhilarating experience of your life, or the most disastrous.

Others call you a control freak. Others call you inflexible. Others despair over your moods, your prickliness, your silence, your black holes. Now you can see them at first hand; now *you* can know the joys of Scorpio. Now you will be on the receiving end; now you may have to take cover from that poisonous tail. Perhaps you will finally understand how truly difficult you can be, why your friends tear their hair out, or why others find you impossible to deal with. Seeing yourself as others see you can be bracing, and in the best of all possible worlds you might learn from your strengths and weaknesses. In the worst, you might decide on permanent withdrawal.

So let's accentuate the positive. You love psychological challenges and unsolved mysteries, so you will have your hands delightedly full. Trying to figure out how to reach your secretive double without setting off alarms will be the first test: A Scorpion will not necessarily trust another Scorpion just because they are both Scorpions. It may think you are prying; it may assume you are seeking control; it may fear that you are trying to horn in on its space. You will have to make the first move in order to gain

trust: If you want a Scorpion to be there
for you, you must be willing to be there
in return. And if you want to be left
alone, you must grant the other the same
privilege. You can either lock pincers in
deadly combat, or you can try to reason
things out. Reason, of course, is not your
forte; but then again, each of you already
knows what the other is thinking and
feeling, so you will have an intuitive head
start. It will not be easy, but if you can

both reach even the slightest accommodation, you might begin to enjoy the
tremendous excitement you obviously
share.

As long as you both keep on moving
together, your frustrations will be side-
tracked and your rages will disappear. So
will your depressions, as each will help
the other out of the dark, pensive caverns
to which you are prone. Then perhaps
you can relax a little and realize that each

of you has finally found a playmate who will do all the insane things you both crave: race car driving, shark hunting, bodysurfing amid coral reefs. Your intense isolation can also come to an end: Now you will have someone who not only understands your highs and lows but feels them as you do. Tremendous electricity is in the offing, but be warned that this duo is *not* for the faint of heart.

Or for the faint of eros. Safely ensconced in the dark, the two of you will uncoil completely; and if your instincts can finally go wild with someone as sensual and passionate as you are, you will explode as you never have before.

Scorpio with Sagittarius

NOVEMBER 23–DECEMBER 21

Sagittarius, the great traveler of the zodiac, is the eternal optimist, the Archer shooting arrows idealistically into the sky. That is exactly the

219

sort of carefree infusion you need.

Few can draw you so easily out of your oppressive pessimism. Few would even try to brave the darker of your many mysterious moods. The Archer, however, can strap you on its back like a knapsack and take off to uncharted terrain, pointing out wonders along the way and chattering like a monkey; and with any luck at all, your worries will disappear. This sign will show you the joys of being spontaneous and free, and introduce you to a thousand people from a hundred fascinating walks of life. Some of them might even be able to help you professionally—so how could there possibly be a downside?

The downside is that you might not even be there. You are extremely controlled, highly emotional, and as moody as the winds—and you like it that way. You have contempt for the Archer's breezy optimism; you scorn the Archer's naked social climbing. Sagittarius can charm the pants off the most suspicious and cynical soul, and not even you are immune; but even as it tries to get you to crack a smile, you are thinking about everything that might go wrong at work; even as it begs you to do something, any-thing, *now*, without thinking, you are looking forward to combing through your books and computer for your next

research project. You have tight sched-
ules to which you cling religiously, so
you cannot feel comfortable doing anything on a whim; and everything you
need, everything that Sagittarius can so
effortlessly provide, you resist with stubborn rectitude. Still, if anyone *can* penetrate that thorny exterior and get you to
relax, have a little fun, and go where the
wind blows (even if only for an hour), it
is the dapper, gregarious Archer. You

would probably be relieved when your spontaneous fun was over, but at least the Archer tried to infuse your life with a little whimsy.

Both of you could benefit, because for all of its breeziness Sagittarius lacks solidity, and you could show the Archer how to take life more seriously. You could also make clear that idealism is useless without a concrete and long-range plan—and that money doesn't grow on trees. Sagittarius, so innocent (and even stupid), will gladly spend before it has earned and blow thousands on its next idyllic vacation. You, however, know the realities of the cruel financial world, and you will make those vacations possible. You will then have the Archer's undying thanks—though you will still have to suffer its self-righteousness now and then. Sagittarius can be a fanatic when it believes itself in the right.

Yet, if you can only unbend a little and slow down the freedom-loving Archer long enough to make a commitment, you could be among the happiest of mortals. And once you decide to express your pleasure in your own sensual way, that eternal wanderer will be glad to stay closer to home.

Scorpio with Capricorn

DECEMBER 22–JANUARY 20

At times this cardinal earth sign, whose symbol is the mountain goat slowly but surely ascending the ladder of success, uncannily may seem to resemble you. Both of you are reserved, very hardworking, and very, very serious. Both of you are materialistic and highly motivated by visions of the money you might accrue, the property you could own, if only things went your way. Both of you are so pessimistic that you doubt that things *will* go your way, but both of you labor on nevertheless. Indeed, both of you so often work overtime that it really won't matter if you only see each other late at night; and because you both have such respect for privacy, you will be happy—sometimes even more than happy—to spend time apart. Each of you fully understands the other's needs and eccentricities; yet despite all of these considerable similarities, your personalities, in other respects, are as different as night and day.

You are emotional and highly charged; Capricorn is pragmatic and slow. You must be passionate about whatever you do in order to give it your best shot; Capricorn, though tireless in its habits, cares not about the job but about the material rewards the job brings. You don't really mind what line of work you ultimately choose because you will always find some aspect of it that excites you; status-obsessed Capricorn requires a prestigious position in order to feel confident and secure. With so many other traits in common, however, none of this will matter much.

You won't even mind that the Goat has little to say, because neither do you. You both only speak when the need arises, so you pay all the more attention when that happens. In many respects this union of like minds will be quiet and dull—which is an astonishing and almost inconceivable thing for a Scorpio. For that reason, it will not be enough to satisfy all of your many needs.

Capricorn is cool, calm, and collected; you always need to explode. When you come home after a long, successful day, you want to work out at the gym or do *something* to satisfy your restless need for physical activity. The Goat, on the contrary, wants only to collapse: turn on the television, relax with you on its arm, forget about its exhausting day. Free time for Capricorn is free time; *free time* for you is time to *do something* . . . or brood. Your temperamental differences may come back to haunt you unless you can find some sort of accommodation.

Perhaps you should try the bedroom, Capricorn's favorite place for savoring its just rewards. The Goat may seem, or even be, dull on the outside, but in the privacy of the boudoir it can simmer with sensuality. Both of you can, therefore, be happy. You can return from your hard day *and* get a good workout; Capricorn can return from its hard day and go straight to bed. Excitement is yours for the taking with this sign, despite all the surface quiet. And once you realize that, you might start coming home early on a regular basis.

Scorpio with Aquarius

JANUARY 21-FEBRUARY 19

Aquarius, *a fixed air* sign symbolized by an angel pouring healing waters over the earth, is the great reformer, the most socially conscious member of the zodiac, always doing its utmost to make the world a better place. You, on the other hand, are so thoroughly self-absorbed that you can never even think about lending your time to a cause or ideal. And it is not that you don't care: You believe very strongly in social issues, and bigotry and injustice make your blood boil. But you become so involved in all of the conflicts you create for yourself that you scarcely have time for anything else. Aquarius has time *only* for others; and that grand humanitarianism, that driving need to solve all the problems confronting the planet, will excite your admiration and respect. But even you, despite all of your passion for solitude and independence, will eventually start to wish that the Water Bearer could spend an occasional night at home.

Dream on. Fund-raisers, caucuses, and political meetings of every sort will take precedence; and although you can hypnotize almost anyone with your piercing eyes, Aquarius will rarely be there to see them. Your mate might scarcely even know who you are—especially since you are difficult to read even for those who take the time. And Aquarius has little of that. You have always desired someone who would respect your fanatical need to be left alone. Now you have it—but the Water Bearer's "respect" almost borders on indifference. Aquarius also is in control. And you find that very hard to accept.

This is one of the few signs whose need for autonomy is as powerful as your own; and as both of you will insist (against no argument) on doing exactly as you wish, you will run little risk of getting in each other's way. That could be a big plus. Each of you, in his own fash- ion, is a powder keg waiting to explode, so the more time you spend apart, the better. But can a relationship thrive on the benefits of separation? What can possibly pull you together?

To begin with, you both firmly believe in your own strong ideals, although yours are largely personal (researching a cure for some unknown disease), and the Water Bearer's are public (fighting to pass some new legislation). Both of you are also idealistic enough to believe that you can always get your way; and although you may run the risk of becoming two immovable objects, your admiration for Aquarius, and the Water Bearer's respect for you, will keep you attracted for some time to come. Both of you need to be endlessly stimulated, so your very differences could become the tie that binds.

But the two of you *must* spend time together, so try a hideaway weekend where no distractions beckon. If Aquarius has no friends clamoring for advice, and you have no books or computer dragging you away, you might finally get to know each other in intimate ways. When that happens, it could be magic. Then it would take a cataclysm to tear you apart.

Scorpio with Pisces

FEBRUARY 20–MARCH 20

*L*ike you, *Pisces is a* water sign (mutable), but instead of being prickly and difficult, it is endlessly gentle and soft.

243

Both of you are needy, insecure, and at the mercy of your uncontrollable emotions, but whereas you are always strong and tempestuous, Pisces is always sweet and apparently confused. Its symbol is two fish swimming in opposite directions, and that wavering uncertainty (or, to your uncompromising mind, lack of direction) may drive you mad. The kindest, most compassionate, most impressionable sign of the zodiac drifts too much with the waves for your taste; and because patience has never been a Scorpion virtue, the empathetic and entrancing Fish may infuriate you—even though its emotional makeup is so curiously similar to yours. You may love adorable Pisces and value its uncanny instincts, yet so much will work against this union that you will have to remind yourself constantly how strong your love really is.

You, after all, are maniacally focused

on everything you do; undisciplined Pisces happily roams from one activity to the next. You require a grand master plan that you can follow to the letter; spontaneous and intuitive Pisces never has any idea where anything will end. You demand form; Pisces rebels against constraints of every sort. You like to build on other people's ideas; Pisces is bursting with originality. You have little imagination; amazingly artistic Pisces explodes with it. Your differences only seem to multiply down the line.

Nevertheless, those differences can mesh; and because both of you are drawn to creative professions, they might even bind you together. The Fish has vision galore, but no concept of follow-through or application. The Fish has talent galore, but insufficient concentration to focus it. You, in every case, will have to be the one to map out a methodical plan, funnel those wonderful abilities, be the master, manager, and stage director. So long as you do so without rancor or cruelty, Pisces will follow your lead.

But you must take care that your obstinate, impatient, and even bitter ways do not force you to say what you will eventually regret. You bristle and lash out when you are hurt or upset; the Fish swims away. It cries easily and cannot bear humiliation, attacks, or even simple unkindness. It would take far less than a poisonous stinger to wound Pisces indelibly, and you could do it in your sleep. One vicious word from you could destroy all of the Fish's questionable confidence, so hold yourself back, or even shut your mouth. If you chase this loving sign away, you will regret it forever. Pisces moves more slowly than you do, but every action and thought comes deep from the heart. If you guide the Fish with affection, you will have the partner of a lifetime.

Pisces, for all of its gentleness, is a wildly sensual sign, and once its lovely eyes begin to shine in your direction, you may—and should—be hooked. Forget your stubbornness and give in: The Fish knows how to salve your wounds. Now these waters can crash from a different kind of tempest.

You and
the
Moon

Just as the Moon takes a month to orbit the Earth, so it requires approximately thirty days to pass through, or transit, the various signs of the zodiac—beginning with Aries, ending with Pisces, and spending about two and a half days in each. As it does so, it exerts an extraordinary influence on our moods, much as it expends a mysterious, physical pull on the ocean's tides.

The Sun may guide our more conscious and overt qualities, but the Moon rules over our instinctive, intuitive life; when we examine our daily moon signs, we become aware of the myriad and mystical ways in which that lunar body affects our emotional weather. When it transits a fire sign, for example, we are often dominated by fiery emotions, such as anger and passion. As it moves to an earth sign, we will feel a more rooted need for stability and comfort. The Moon in a water sign will generally bring watery emotions, like sadness and confusion; and an air-sign passage will lead to a sharpening of our thirst for knowledge.

Obviously, emotional weather isn't identical for everyone; the relationship between the position of the Moon and your particular sun sign will influence what the precise mood of the moment will be for you, and a constant subtle interplay occurs. If we pay close attention to the passages of the Moon, however, we can become far more adept at negotiating wisely and well the many challenges and changes of our daily life.

(Consult the moon charts beginning on page 332 for the time and date that the Moon enters each of the twelve signs of the zodiac throughout every month of the year from 1997 to 2005.)

The Moon in Aries

When the Moon tra-verses aggressive, impetuous, and enthu-siastic Aries, you may find yourself even more focused on work than ever before. Because you are a natural perfectionist, this transit will only make you more compulsive and zealous about doing your best. The strain of the next few days could take a toll on your health, however, so you should try to lighten up and take breaks. Stress headaches, eye-strain, sore shoulders, and backaches are possible, if not indeed likely, but if you work out in the gym, or play sports aggressively with your friends, or even run mindlessly around a track, you might be able to relieve enough pressure to allay them. You might also take a sauna or get a deep-body massage to iron out all those kinks.

Your workaholic nature and consistent frugality should alleviate any money worries you might have, and your nest egg, during this transit, will be safe. Indeed, you should feel so monetarily secure during this passage that you might want to explore new venues for investing your profits. You run little chance of squandering them away.

If you are single, you may have to drag yourself from your desk in order to meet anyone; yet it is also possible that your dream date could be working in the next office or lingering down the hall. Keep your eyes open and stop gloating over the financial killing you are about to make, or you might miss the romantic opportunity of a lifetime. When the potential love of your life walks through the door, you should be prepared.

If you are already attached, this would be a good time for the two of you to withdraw some of your savings and finally make that big purchase you have been talking about for so long. Chances are that even if you do make a down payment on a house or car, you might still have enough left over to buy something frivolous. Don't feel guilty about rewarding yourself for all of your hard work: Once the Moon enters possessive and materialistic Taurus, you will once again start pinching pennies. So take advantage while you can: build a swimming pool, book your dream vacation, go on a photographic safari. Everything will slow down considerably under the coming Taurus Moon.

The Moon in Taurus

The Moon *is exalted,*

or at its strongest, in Venus-ruled Taurus, so now you can put your ambitions on the back burner for a few days and enjoy the peaceful rewards of this lazy and amorous sign. Not only will this transit add stability to your life, but you will also become far more sensitive to the needs of others. Instead of telling those who seek your support to wait until the workday is through, you might put your own tasks aside temporarily to lend a helping hand. This new, unselfish you may surprise even your closest family members and friends; now that your temper is suddenly under control, and you feel better about things in general, you might try making amends if you've had a recent falling-out with a friend, relative, or colleague.

Taurus is a financially stable sign, so during this transit you can accomplish any monetary goal you want to if you put your mind to it. This would be an excellent time to plan for the future, because the influence of this sensible Moon will allow you to invest wisely.

If you are single and looking for a serious relationship, the sensual Taurus transit could do the trick. Indeed, because your usual suspiciousness will fly straight out the window, you will uncharacteristically see good and attractive qualities in everyone you meet—so much so, indeed, that you might find yourself attracted to one person too many. It would be better for you, however, to gravitate to someone whose practicality and desire for monetary security resemble your own. And don't worry if you grow confused: The upcoming Gemini Moon is cynical and aloof, so if you are unsure of your options at the present moment, the right choice will quickly become apparent.

If you are already attached, the two of you could scarcely ask for a better influence: Now is a splendid time to renew the feelings that brought you together in the first place. It doesn't matter what you do: Go out on the town, relax at home with a romantic video, spend the entire evening preparing a lavish gourmet meal. You have both looked forward to this throughout the grueling day, so pour some champagne, turn on the mood music, and prepare to cap it all off. This is the ultimate Moon for making love.

The Moon in Gemini

Y*ou, who love the chal-*lenge of beginning new projects, will be thrilled under the influence of this mercantile Moon. All of your plans will come alive, and wheeling and dealing will be the motivating force that keeps them creative and fresh. Money may be no object, but you still must exercise a certain amount of restraint: Don't run wild, and don't fling dollars away on every hare-brained scheme that crosses your desk. Reason will be emphasized during this transit, so rely on good sense and discrimination for a few days rather than the emotions—especially when it comes to spending money. If anything can threaten your peace of mind during this passage, it is dipping into your pocket-book unnecessarily. Caution will reassert itself during the upcoming Cancer Moon. For now, get a tight grip on your impulses.

You may feel a little hyperactive over the next few days, and a great deal of anger may brew, but arguing with your colleagues would not be the best way to release it. Instead, go swimming, hiking, bike riding, jogging: Do anything you must to burn off steam. Your physical desires will be at their peak during this transit, so if you don't live near a park or an outdoor track, visit a health club. Those who do not relieve the pressure and channel their abundant energy constructively could go haywire and start making bad decisions.

If you are single, you might even find someone interesting at the gym. Actually, you will find interesting people everywhere. Gemini is a very versatile, talkative, and social sign, so you will be able to strike up relationships and conversations galore—which you usually find difficult, if not impossible. You can very quickly learn whether or not the two of you have anything in common; and as soon as the emotional Cancer Moon comes into view, you will know for certain if you can really fulfill each other's needs.

If you are already committed, you and your partner may finally start discussing all those issues you have been setting aside for a rainy day. Now is the perfect time because conversation will simply flow; and if the two of you can reasonably discuss your differences without getting into volatile arguments, you may find yourself pleasantly renewing more delightful and romantic feelings.

The Moon in Cancer

The Moon rules Can-
cer and feels remarkably at home there,
so all of your deepest instincts will be
heightened during this transit. You and
Cancer already have much in common

(both secretive, insecure, and highly emotional water signs), and when your caution meets the Crab's defensiveness, you might find it almost impossible to lower your guard and share what you feel with anyone. You may cling to old grudges and once again start to feel that the entire world is against you, and depression will be a distinct danger.

You will also feel wary at work, so you had better be prepared to go it alone (which you like doing in any case) until you relearn how to accept assistance from those closest to you. The people around you, both on the job and at home, only want to make your life easier and not control it, but you may not be able to accept that until the Moon transits confident, boisterous Leo. Wait a few days before making any important personal or professional moves.

If you are single and secretly hope to

meet someone special, you will have to make an effort to be less suspicious and distrustful of everyone you meet. You may find it hard to believe that anyone else can truly care, especially now, but the only way you are ever going to let someone in is to open the door. You *can* trust certain people, despite all of your pessimism; and if you can believe that, your dream date may suddenly appear out of nowhere. Chance favors the prepared mind. You may not understand the attraction, but it doesn't matter: When the amorous Leo Moon rolls around, you will know for certain whether you have made the right decision or not.

If you are already committed, you will want to spend as much time as you can with your loved ones. Staying at home, enjoying family dinners, and simply talking (especially about whatever you have not had time to discuss recently) will be the perfect antidote to a long hard day at work. This is a very family-minded Moon, so you will once again be reminded how much you enjoy the company of your loved ones. And those happy evenings should lead easily to passionate, fun-filled nights with your true love.

The Moon in Leo

When the Moon enters confident, jubilant, and ostentatious Leo, the world will suddenly burst with energy and color, and you will be noticed wherever you go. That may bother you at first because you are so private, but under this sunny influence, your personality cannot help shining. Not only will your more extroverted side, which usually remains hidden, come to the fore, but your professional life will be more sharply focused. You will suddenly be able to accomplish anything you want: Ask for a promotion, quit your present job, start up a new business, strike out on your own. Leo is ruled by the Sun, and brilliant rays will effusively pour down.

Your friends may flock to you: They will sense somehow that you can steer them to the excitement they crave. Your vitality at a maximum, you will require—and want—very little sleep. But your lavishness will also be heightened, so you will have to be on guard against spending sprees. The king of the jungle loves luxury, and this Moon will make you want to surround yourself with plenty of expensive and glamorous items.

If you are single and want to attract a new love interest, this is the time. Almost everyone you meet will feel as exuberant as you do, and your unwontedly glowing personality should finish off the trick. The real test, however, will come next: When the Moon transits modest and self-conscious Virgo, introspection will again take over, and fun-loving extroversion will be a thing of the past. If you can still hold your new love's interest then, it will be the real thing indeed.

If you are already attached, you may find that professional obligations will play havoc with the schedule the two of you have set up, so your partner will have to evince patience while you bask in your success over the next few days. But be careful: Your needs will almost certainly come first during this self-centered passage, but don't forget the person with whom you have been sharing your life. Include your partner in social activities, and you may be pleasantly surprised at how well the mood continues as you un-latch the door at home. If so, then don't even think about how tired you are: Sleep can come later. Prepare instead for a night of passion you are unlikely ever to forget.

The Moon in Virgo

When the Moon tran-sits self-conscious, restless, and high-strung Virgo, you can once again give in to introversion and retreat from the many friends and professional acquaintances who demanded (but also gave you) so much over the last few days. This is the time to gather your thoughts and look at yourself with a clear eye, but don't be too critical or harsh. Virgo and you, the great perfectionists of the zodiac, are rarely satisfied with anything, so you will have to remind yourself constantly that there is more to life than failure. Instead of putting yourself down for what lies outside your control, use this opportunity to recognize—and over-come—your weaknesses.

Especially after the extravagance of the last transit, this should be a fruitful financial period. You tend toward frugality in any case, so you will have a tendency to scrimp and save. Invest your money wisely now, and you can spend it more lavishly later on. Virgo is a very health-conscious sign, so this will also be an excellent time to get into physical shape and release all the anxiety and stress that will probably plague you more than usual.

Meeting someone new could be difficult under Virgo because caution and suspicion will probably overpower any inklings of trust you may feel. Don't wait for bells to ring and butterflies to appear in your stomach; if you meet someone you like, have a serious conversation. Share your hopes and dreams for the future and explore the possibilities. Get to know each other well. When the amorous and marriage-minded Libra Moon comes around, you can then investigate any romantic feelings that may have cropped up.

If you are already attached, take care that you and your mate do not hurl insults at each other or sit across the dinner table criticizing every action and thought. If both of you are feeling touchy, which is likely, then tell your spouse you need to be alone. Mull over your discontentments without speaking them aloud. If you can retreat without feeling guilty, you may be able to reignite your passion; and if you are gentle rather than demanding, your mate might provide a seductive invitation at the evening's end. If not, don't worry: With the Libra Moon on the horizon, romance will be prominent once again.

The Moon in Libra

Romance is in the air when the Moon transits amorous, harmonious, and artistic Libra, which is ruled by the goddess of love. So, however, is laziness, which you may find difficult to deal with. Yet, if you start pushing your physical limits, you will only become more frustrated still; and what matters most during this transit is learning to relax. Accept the fact that you may not be as productive as usual, and join the social whirl instead. Libra excels at networking, so now you should accept all those invitations you previously disregarded. The Moon will soon enough enter your own sign, and then your drive and ambition will return in spades.

Extravagance, indulgence, and frivolity are almost synonymous with the Libra Moon, so be certain to keep your spending in check over the next few days. Temptation will be rife, but so is your natural inclination to frugality. Heed the latter; take a deep breath and remind yourself how much (or how little) money is available to you at the present time.

The Libra transit is the zodiac's

most marriage-minded sign, so if you would like to change your single status, this is the best of all possible Moons. But keep in mind that falling in love will be easy now—possibly even too easy—and that you run the risk of becoming infatuated with the *idea* of romantic magic and not with an actual person. You can be swept off your feet by someone who offers you compliments and promises of love, affection, and financial security, but who may not satisfy you in the long run. Use your head instead of your heart . . . and wait a few days until the Moon transits caustic Scorpio. Then you can rely with greater confidence on your judgment.

If you are already committed, warn your partner that you may be low on energy for the next few days and that you might want to be left alone. It is very possible that he or she may be feeling amorous during this passage, so make every effort to reassure your mate that this is only a passing mood and that it should not be taken personally. Once the Moon enters your own sign, your energy will reappear as if by magic, and your libido will be fully restored.

The Moon in Scorpio

The Moon is fallen, or most weakened, in Pluto-ruled Scorpio, so now you may run your entire gamut of emotions, from ecstasy to misery to towering rage, in a matter of days.

If it sounds confusing to you, imagine what it must be like for those closest to you, whether at home or at work. Indeed, your smarter or more experienced friends will probably not even phone you until the next transit; and although your tremendous drive and innovative ideas may help nail down a creative project or high-stakes financial deal, this is not the time to attempt cooperation with others. You are in the driver's seat, and anything

less than complete control will be re-
jected out of hand.

Because you are working under enormous pressure and at breakneck speed,
your colleagues will probably be happy to
stay away; and if you can be left alone to
pursue your own interests, you will not
only come up with wildly exciting initia-
tives but moneymakers to boot. Though
your finances should be excellent, you
might try waiting until the Moon transits

optimistic Sagittarius to invest: Then you will more easily part with your money.

If you are single but think you have finally found your dream mate, follow your instincts. Because you are naturally suspicious of everyone you meet, whoever manages to hold your interest beyond the initial meeting must have something. You may indeed have found the one. If so, and if you let your guard down just a little, you might even discover a capacity for fun that you either didn't know existed or hadn't explored in months—or years.

If you are already attached, your partner should be warned in no uncertain terms, that the next few days could be among the most passionate of your lives, but also, potentially among the most unpleasant. A Scorpion under Scorpio is a walking keg of dynamite: At any time, at even the slightest touch, it might explode . . . and blow up an entire town. Don't insist on having your own way all the time, or you will be inviting disaster. Instead, be sensible: Go dancing, see a film, take a drive to some special place where the two of you can do something memorable. And let passion, by all means, spotlight the days *and* nights.

The Moon in Sagittarius

Y*ou can take a deep* breath now that the perilous journey through Scorpio is over, and the Moon has entered the most serendipitous, but also the most wasteful, sign of the zodiac. Your sobriety and hard work will fall by the wayside as you will be showered with too many social invitations to refuse. Instead of fighting them, join in. You may be shy in public and detest crowds, but if you concentrate on the professional networking that these social events entail, you cannot help but gain.

You will have a gilded touch during this transit and may be bombarded by professional opportunities, financial re-

wards, and a general feeling of content-
ment as exhilarating as it is rare. Try your
luck by taking up a new sport or competitive game: tennis, track, swimming, hiking, chess, whatever it may be. You may
even decide to plunge and buy a lottery
ticket, or go to a casino for some light-
hearted gambling. Rarely do you feel so
spirited or optimistic, but exercise a little
caution. The Sagittarius Moon can be *too*
optimistic, and it may fill you with unre-

alistic expectations that are sure to come crashing down under Capricorn.

Beware, therefore, if you begin to date a variety of people. This can be a wonderfully fortuitous Moon, especially for business, or even for incidental introductions to prospective business contacts, but it can also be treacherously hopeful and false, especially in love. Your chances are by no means dire, but if you are looking for someone who shares your dreams, it is possible that you will simply fantasize and trick yourself into believing that the person currently gazing into your eyes is the one. Rather than get lost in a self-created maze of unfulfilled expectations, try to be realistic with yourself and especially with others who may want to get close to you.

If you are already committed, you and your mate might be pleasantly surprised at how healthy your bank account appears. Sagittarius is the great traveler of the zodiac, so this would be the perfect time to spread the travel brochures on the table and spend an evening choosing the best place to go for a dream vacation you will never forget. So long as you make those plans during this lucky Moon, you will never regret your choice.

The Moon in Capricorn

The Moon is detrimen-tal, or not very comfortable, in Saturn-ruled Capricorn, so you should feel thoroughly at home: reserved, hardworking, and persevering as always. The Sagittarius

Moon, though splendidly jovial and optimistic, made you feel unnatural, because lightness of spirit is something you can neither understand nor get used to, but now you can go back to long hours and super-sobriety. In other words, you will be your usual grumpy self during the Capricorn Moon.

When intense Scorpio meets ambitious Capricorn, no one can impede the laserlike focus and intensity you will bring to everything you do. You may spend early mornings and late nights at work for the next couple of days. But this is also a Moon of trust, so now would be an excellent time to get to know the neighbors a little better, take a greater interest in the environment, or even start eating healthier foods that could revive your energy. Family re-unions, in which you finally work out age-old differences, may also be in the offing, whether you like them or not.

On the other hand, getting to know someone new during this serious transit could prove difficult: Your pessimism and sobriety could be off-putting or even intimidating to those unable or unwilling to confront that type of intensity, especially on a first date. But at least this person would see you as you really are. It is also possible, however, that you will meet someone as pensive as you are, whose ambitions match your own aspirations and dreams. In that case have patience, because the upcoming Aquarius Moon is extremely talkative and social. You may clam up and fortify your defenses today, but tomorrow you will let your guard down and breathe again.

If you are already committed, you should warn your mate that your temporary moodiness might incline you to hole up in your office for the next few days, and that, at very least, you will be even less communicative than usual and may fall entirely silent for hours at a time. Neither of these options will come as a surprise to a Scorpion mate, who should be used to your ups and downs. But it is also possible that, now more than ever, you will want your partner to pull you out from under. If so, say so; and push even harder to leave your work behind you. Once in the sanctity of your home

(especially, perhaps, the bedroom), open-
ing the sensual doors may be the best
way to communicate after a long and
grueling day.

The Moon in Aquarius

Be prepared for a calendar filled with endless activity when the Moon rolls through the most social, high-strung, and innovative sign of the zodiac. You may wish you could stay in bed throughout this transit because you stand little chance of controlling your life for the next few days.

Aquarius is extraordinarily open and willing to try anything new, so friends you haven't seen in ages will now arrive on your doorstep; social engagements you have been avoiding for months will suddenly become imperative, and your generosity and hospitality may be tested to the utmost by someone in the throes of a crisis who will call on you for endless support. You will be forced to divide your time between saying "no" (which is your usual preference) and helping out those in need, so you might as well accept the fact and get on with it. To your surprise, it won't kill you. And indeed, under the influence of this most altruistic of Moons, you might actually find that thinking of others before yourself can be even more rewarding than you ever dreamed possible.

Meeting someone new, if you are in the market, will be a cinch because everywhere you turn there will be a party, gathering, political rally, or work-related activity crying for your attention. Because you are usually too shy and too wrapped up in your own concerns to take the first step, this would be the ideal time to ask a friend to make an introduction; and because everyone around you will appear bubbly and vivacious, some of that light-some magic might even rub off on you. If so, you should prove to be a wonderful dinner companion.

If you are already attached, the fundamental conflict you feel throughout this transit will be intensified. Though your mate may want to get out of the house, you will be torn between playing the social animal and retreating into your secure bubble. This is the time for compromise, unpleasant though it may be, and in fact you may find yourself wanting to exalt your partner's desires over your own, wanting to make his or her wishes your command. Be prepared to see friends, play cards, go to the latest film or play. When nighttime falls, you may get your way—and endless private pleasures will once again prevail.

The Moon in Pisces

You *are rarely accused* of thinking with your heart and not your head, but you will be now. When the Moon transits the most impressionable, intuitive, and fantasy-filled sign of the zodiac, you will not only be more sensitive to friends, family, and colleagues, but you will even discover your own eloquence. Exactly the right words will flow at any given time, but you will also be extremely hypersensitive and may overreact by misinterpreting everything that anyone says.

Creativity will be the best antidote to any stress that may assail you, and if you are not currently in the midst of a project that calls on your deepest imaginative resources, now is the time to start. Writing, drawing, dancing, indeed any activity that de-emphasizes analytical prowess, will be a plus. But watch yourself even then. You are used to being in tight control of your senses and emotions, but the flowing Pisces Moon will force you to spontaneity. Instead of doing what is necessary, you will merely do what feels good. This will be a novel experience, so although you may enjoy the many parties to which you are invited, take it easy and don't indulge too much.

If you are single, your wonderful spirits will make you that much keener to welcome a new romantic interest into your life; and under the spell of this magical Moon, you may be tempted to swoon over anyone who crosses your path. If you are willing to reveal the feelings you usually bottle tightly inside, over the next few days you will probably meet others who are just as receptive and infatuated with life as you are.

If you are already attached, you and your partner may fall in love all over again. You cannot wait to be alone in the dark and will have to exercise all your patience to keep from throwing your visitors out. The two of you may gush and coo wherever you go; and however disgusting that may be to others, it will be a thrill for you. Act on it: Stop whatever you are doing and rush home. Pop open a bottle of champagne, dim the lights, and play some romantic music. The inimitable Pisces Moon will take care of the rest, and a long, passionate night will then unfold.

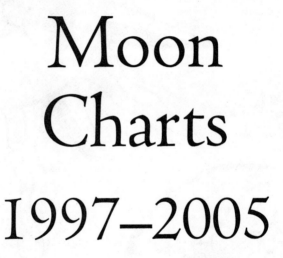

Moon
Charts
1997–2005

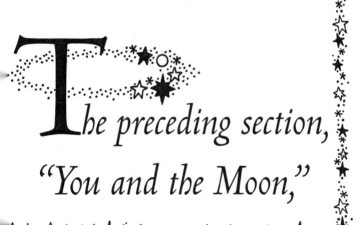

The preceding section, "You and the Moon,"

explained in detail how the Moon affects your emotions and behavior as it moves through the twelve signs of the zodiac. It takes approximately thirty days for the Moon to pass through, or transit, the twelve signs—spending about two and a half days in each. So every month, for the short period that the Moon is moving through Leo, or Aries, or Scorpio (or any other sign), you can take advantage of the Moon's positive or negative influences.

The following charts show the date
and time the Moon enters each sign of
the zodiac. Just look up the current date
(charts are provided for the years 1997
through 2005); the sign that precedes the
date indicates the Moon's current transit.
For instance, in the two following transits

Can Jan 10 19:43

Leo Jan 13 02:45

the Moon enters the sign of Cancer on

January 10 at 19:43 (7:43 P.M.) and stays in that sign until entering the sign of Leo on January 13 at 02:45 (2:45 A.M.). All times are eastern standard time in a twenty-four-hour clock format: 00:01–12:00 (noon) are the A.M. hours; 12:01–24:00 (midnight) are the P.M. hours (from 13:00 to 24:00, subtract 12 to translate into P.M.).

1997

	Sag Feb 01 23:49	Aqu Mar 05 14:53
Sco Jan 03 08:00	Cap Feb 04 03:43	Pis Mar 07 14:56
Sag Jan 05 14:26	Aqu Feb 06 04:20	Ari Mar 09 14:32
Cap Jan 07 16:54	Pis Feb 08 03:33	Tau Mar 11 15:38
Aqu Jan 09 16:59	Ari Feb 10 03:29	Gem Mar 13 19:49
Pis Jan 11 16:50	Tau Feb 12 05:56	Can Mar 16 03:51
Ari Jan 13 18:21	Gem Feb 14 11:54	Leo Mar 18 15:08
Tau Jan 15 22:40	Can Feb 16 21:12	Vir Mar 21 03:59
Gem Jan 18 05:53	Leo Feb 19 08:52	Lib Mar 23 16:34
Can Jan 20 15:28	Vir Feb 21 21:38	Sco Mar 26 03:41
Leo Jan 23 02:50	Lib Feb 24 10:22	Sag Mar 28 12:38
Vir Jan 25 15:26	Sco Feb 26 21:55	Cap Mar 30 19:06
Lib Jan 28 04:21	Sag Mar 01 07:00	Aqu Apr 01 22:57
Sco Jan 30 15:47	Cap Mar 03 12:37	Pis Apr 04 00:41

Ari Apr 06 01:19	Gem May 07 15:21	Leo Jun 08 14:58
Tau Apr 08 02:21	Can May 09 21:13	Vir Jun 11 02:43
Gem Apr 10 05:27	Leo May 12 06:32	Lib Jun 13 15:35
Can Apr 12 12:04	Vir May 14 18:43	Sco Jun 16 02:50
Leo Apr 14 22:22	Lib May 17 07:26	Sag Jun 18 10:37
Vir Apr 17 11:00	Sco May 19 18:11	Cap Jun 20 15:01
Lib Apr 19 23:35	Sag May 22 01:49	Aqu Jun 22 17:20
Sco Apr 22 10:17	Cap May 24 06:50	Pis Jun 24 19:08
Sag Apr 24 18:31	Aqu May 26 10:19	Ari Jun 26 21:38
Cap Apr 27 00:31	Pis May 28 13:17	Tau Jun 29 01:23
Aqu Apr 29 04:49	Ari May 30 16:17	Gem Jul 01 06:35
Pis May 01 07:49	Tau Jun 01 19:39	Can Jul 03 13:33
Ari May 03 09:59	Gem Jun 03 23:55	Leo Jul 05 22:45
Tau May 05 12:04	Can Jun 06 06:01	Vir Jul 08 10:22

Lib Jul 10 23:20	Sag Aug 12 04:44	Aqu Sep 12 23:08
Sco Jul 13 11:19	Cap Aug 14 10:40	Pis Sep 14 23:58
Sag Jul 15 20:01	Aqu Aug 16 12:57	Ari Sep 16 23:25
Cap Jul 18 00:44	Pis Aug 18 13:00	Tau Sep 18 23:22
Aqu Jul 20 02:28	Ari Aug 20 12:45	Gem Sep 21 01:39
Pis Jul 22 02:59	Tau Aug 22 13:58	Can Sep 23 07:33
Ari Jul 24 04:03	Gem Aug 24 17:56	Leo Sep 25 17:12
Tau Jul 26 06:53	Can Aug 27 01:11	Vir Sep 28 05:27
Gem Jul 28 12:04	Leo Aug 29 11:19	Lib Sep 30 18:32
Can Jul 30 19:38	Vir Aug 31 23:27	Sco Oct 03 06:57
Leo Aug 02 05:26	Lib Sep 03 12:29	Sag Oct 05 17:42
Vir Aug 04 17:15	Sco Sep 06 01:08	Cap Oct 08 02:02
Lib Aug 07 06:16	Sag Sep 08 11:53	Aqu Oct 10 07:28
Sco Aug 09 18:49	Cap Sep 10 19:22	Pis Oct 12 09:58

Ari Oct 14 10:24	Gem Nov 14 22:05	Leo Dec 16 17:57
Tau Oct 16 10:16	Can Nov 17 01:33	Vir Dec 19 03:59
Gem Oct 18 11:27	Leo Nov 19 08:38	Lib Dec 21 16:34
Can Oct 20 15:45	Vir Nov 21 19:32	Sco Dec 24 05:06
Leo Oct 23 00:10	Lib Nov 24 08:29	Sag Dec 26 15:06
Vir Oct 25 11:59	Sco Nov 26 20:42	Cap Dec 28 21:47
Lib Oct 28 01:04	Sag Nov 29 06:28	Aqu Dec 31 01:57
Sco Oct 30 13:14	Cap Dec 01 13:37	
Sag Nov 01 23:25	Aqu Dec 03 18:57	**1998**
Cap Nov 04 07:30	Pis Dec 05 23:06	Pis Jan 02 04:55
Aqu Nov 06 13:32	Ari Dec 08 02:23	Ari Jan 04 07:43
Pis Nov 08 17:34	Tau Dec 10 04:59	Tau Jan 06 10:52
Ari Nov 10 19:43	Gem Dec 12 07:35	Gem Jan 08 14:42
Tau Nov 12 20:45	Can Dec 14 11:25	Can Jan 10 19:43

Leo Jan 13 02:45	Lib Feb 14 08:17	Sag Mar 18 15:55
Vir Jan 15 12:31	Sco Feb 16 21:12	Cap Mar 21 01:41
Lib Jan 18 00:44	Sag Feb 19 08:55	Aqu Mar 23 08:00
Sco Jan 20 13:33	Cap Feb 21 17:29	Pis Mar 25 10:41
Sag Jan 23 00:23	Aqu Feb 23 22:08	Ari Mar 27 10:48
Cap Jan 25 07:38	Pis Feb 25 23:41	Tau Mar 29 10:06
Aqu Jan 27 11:25	Ari Feb 27 23:42	Gem Mar 31 10:38
Pis Jan 29 13:07	Tau Mar 02 00:01	Can Apr 02 14:10
Ari Jan 31 14:21	Gem Mar 04 02:15	Leo Apr 04 21:36
Tau Feb 02 16:24	Can Mar 06 07:26	Vir Apr 07 08:25
Gem Feb 04 20:09	Leo Mar 08 15:45	Lib Apr 09 21:04
Can Feb 07 01:57	Vir Mar 11 02:35	Sco Apr 12 09:55
Leo Feb 09 09:57	Lib Mar 13 14:57	Sag Apr 14 21:51
Vir Feb 11 20:09	Sco Mar 16 03:50	Cap Apr 17 08:04

Aqu Apr 19 15:40	Ari May 21 06:05	Gem Jun 21 16:26
Pis Apr 21 20:04	Tau May 23 07:05	Can Jun 23 18:38
Ari Apr 23 21:29	Gem May 25 07:25	Leo Jun 25 23:04
Tau Apr 25 21:08	Can May 27 08:59	Vir Jun 28 06:54
Gem Apr 27 20:55	Leo May 29 13:39	Lib Jun 30 18:04
Can Apr 29 22:58	Vir May 31 22:21	Sco Jul 03 06:45
Leo May 02 04:49	Lib Jun 03 10:16	Sag Jul 05 18:23
Vir May 04 14:47	Sco Jun 05 23:04	Cap Jul 08 03:26
Lib May 07 03:18	Sag Jun 08 10:33	Aqu Jul 10 09:51
Sco May 09 16:09	Cap Jun 10 19:49	Pis Jul 12 14:21
Sag May 12 03:47	Aqu Jun 13 03:02	Ari Jul 14 17:44
Cap May 14 13:37	Pis Jun 15 08:30	Tau Jul 16 20:33
Aqu May 16 21:29	Ari Jun 17 12:22	Gem Jul 18 23:18
Pis May 19 03:02	Tau Jun 19 14:47	Can Jul 21 02:43

Leo Jul 23 07:48	Lib Aug 24 10:02	Sag Sep 25 18:04
Vir Jul 25 15:34	Sco Aug 26 22:25	Cap Sep 28 05:29
Lib Jul 28 02:14	Sag Aug 29 10:54	Aqu Sep 30 13:51
Sco Jul 30 14:44	Cap Aug 31 21:21	Pis Oct 02 18:22
Sag Aug 02 02:47	Aqu Sep 03 04:19	Ari Oct 04 19:31
Cap Aug 04 12:16	Pis Sep 05 07:46	Tau Oct 06 18:57
Aqu Aug 06 18:30	Ari Sep 07 08:52	Gem Oct 08 18:43
Pis Aug 08 22:03	Tau Sep 09 09:16	Can Oct 10 20:49
Ari Aug 11 00:09	Gem Sep 11 10:40	Leo Oct 13 02:25
Tau Aug 13 02:04	Can Sep 13 14:20	Vir Oct 15 11:32
Gem Aug 15 04:45	Leo Sep 15 20:48	Lib Oct 17 23:02
Can Aug 17 08:55	Vir Sep 18 05:51	Sco Oct 20 11:36
Leo Aug 19 15:00	Lib Sep 20 16:57	Sag Oct 23 00:15
Vir Aug 21 23:21	Sco Sep 23 05:21	Cap Oct 25 12:03

Aqu Oct 27 21:42	Ari Nov 28 15:32	Gem Dec 30 02:21
Pis Oct 30 03:57	Tau Nov 30 16:51	
Ari Nov 01 06:26	Gem Dec 02 16:29	**1999**
Tau Nov 03 06:11	Can Dec 04 16:27	Can Jan 01 03:15
Gem Nov 05 05:10	Leo Dec 06 18:55	Leo Jan 03 05:30
Can Nov 07 05:39	Vir Dec 09 01:22	Vir Jan 05 10:50
Leo Nov 09 09:33	Lib Dec 11 11:43	Lib Jan 07 19:52
Vir Nov 11 17:36	Sco Dec 14 00:16	Sco Jan 10 07:48
Lib Nov 14 04:57	Sag Dec 16 12:46	Sag Jan 12 20:22
Sco Nov 16 17:40	Cap Dec 18 23:54	Cap Jan 15 07:27
Sag Nov 19 06:12	Aqu Dec 21 09:15	Aqu Jan 17 16:10
Cap Nov 21 17:44	Pis Dec 23 16:44	Pis Jan 19 22:39
Aqu Nov 24 03:42	Ari Dec 25 22:02	Ari Jan 22 03:24
Pis Nov 26 11:12	Tau Dec 28 01:03	Tau Jan 24 06:51

Gem Jan 26 09:28	Leo Feb 26 22:44	Lib Mar 30 20:49
Can Jan 28 11:56	Vir Mar 01 05:04	Sco Apr 02 07:48
Leo Jan 30 15:16	Lib Mar 03 13:34	Sag Apr 04 20:07
Vir Feb 01 20:37	Sco Mar 06 00:22	Cap Apr 07 08:38
Lib Feb 04 04:55	Sag Mar 08 12:45	Aqu Apr 09 19:23
Sco Feb 06 16:06	Cap Mar 11 00:52	Pis Apr 12 02:33
Sag Feb 09 04:37	Aqu Mar 13 10:30	Ari Apr 14 05:45
Cap Feb 11 16:09	Pis Mar 15 16:29	Tau Apr 16 06:06
Aqu Feb 14 00:55	Ari Mar 17 19:12	Gem Apr 18 05:38
Pis Feb 16 06:39	Tau Mar 19 20:08	Can Apr 20 06:27
Ari Feb 18 10:05	Gem Mar 21 21:05	Leo Apr 22 10:06
Tau Feb 20 12:28	Can Mar 23 23:34	Vir Apr 24 17:03
Gem Feb 22 14:53	Leo Mar 26 04:22	Lib Apr 27 02:46
Can Feb 24 18:08	Vir Mar 28 11:34	Sco Apr 29 14:12

Sag May 02 02:35	Aqu Jun 03 08:35	Tau Jul 07 10:20
Cap May 04 15:11	Ari Jun 08 00:06	Gem Jul 09 11:58
Aqu May 07 02:39	Tau Jun 10 02:42	Can Jul 11 12:27
Pis May 09 11:14	Gem Jun 12 02:47	Leo Jul 13 13:26
Ari May 11 15:51	Can Jun 14 02:14	Vir Jul 15 16:38
Tau May 13 16:55	Leo Jun 16 03:07	Lib Jul 17 23:20
Gem May 15 16:07	Vir Jun 18 07:12	Sco Jul 20 09:30
Can May 17 15:39	Lib Jun 20 15:10	Sag Jul 22 21:47
Leo May 19 17:36	Sco Jun 23 02:17	Cap Jul 25 10:07
Vir May 21 23:16	Sag Jun 25 14:50	Aqu Jul 27 20:53
Lib May 24 08:29	Cap Jun 28 03:10	Pis Jul 30 05:26
Sco May 26 20:04	Aqu Jun 30 14:18	Ari Aug 01 11:45
Sag May 29 08:36	Pis Jul 02 23:33	Tau Aug 05 18:56
Cap May 31 21:04	Ari Jul 05 06:20	Can Aug 07 20:52

Leo Aug 09 22:55	Lib Sep 10 17:15	Sag Oct 12 21:18
Vir Aug 12 02:21	Sco Sep 13 02:08	Cap Oct 15 10:02
Lib Aug 14 08:24	Sag Sep 15 13:34	Aqu Oct 17 22:15
Sco Aug 16 17:39	Cap Sep 18 02:12	Pis Oct 20 07:31
Sag Aug 19 05:31	Aqu Sep 20 13:36	Ari Oct 22 12:39
Cap Aug 21 17:59	Pis Sep 22 21:49	Tau Oct 24 14:24
Aqu Aug 24 04:48	Ari Sep 25 02:32	Gem Oct 26 14:33
Pis Aug 26 12:48	Tau Sep 27 04:49	Can Oct 28 15:09
Ari Aug 28 18:08	Gem Sep 29 06:20	Leo Oct 30 17:46
Tau Aug 30 21:39	Can Oct 01 08:31	Vir Nov 01 23:07
Gem Sep 02 00:24	Leo Oct 03 12:13	Lib Nov 04 06:56
Can Sep 04 03:09	Vir Oct 05 17:39	Sco Nov 06 16:45
Leo Sep 06 06:28	Lib Oct 08 00:51	Sag Nov 09 04:14
Vir Sep 08 10:56	Sco Oct 10 10:01	Cap Nov 11 16:59

Aqu Nov 14 05:44	Ari Dec 16 07:28	Ari Jan 12 13:46
Pis Nov 16 16:19	Tau Dec 18 11:43	Tau Jan 14 19:36
Ari Nov 18 22:55	Gem Dec 20 12:37	Gem Jan 16 22:23
Tau Nov 21 01:24	Can Dec 22 11:52	Can Jan 18 23:00
Gem Nov 23 01:13	Leo Dec 24 11:32	Leo Jan 20 22:58
Can Nov 25 00:29	Vir Dec 26 13:34	Vir Jan 23 00:07
Leo Nov 27 01:19	Lib Dec 28 19:14	Lib Jan 25 04:09
Vir Nov 29 05:10	Sco Dec 31 04:36	Sco Jan 27 12:01
Lib Dec 01 12:29		Sag Jan 29 23:17
Sco Dec 03 22:35	*2000*	Cap Feb 01 12:09
Sag Dec 06 10:27	Sag Jan 02 16:31	Aqu Feb 04 00:30
Cap Dec 08 23:12	Cap Jan 05 05:23	Pis Feb 06 11:00
Aqu Dec 11 11:57	Aqu Jan 07 17:52	Ari Feb 08 19:16
Pis Dec 13 23:15	Pis Jan 10 04:58	Tau Feb 11 01:19

Gem Feb 13 05:22	Leo Mar 15 16:42	Lib Apr 16 07:35
Can Feb 15 07:44	Vir Mar 17 19:48	Sco Apr 18 14:35
Leo Feb 17 09:11	Lib Mar 19 23:57	Sag Apr 20 23:57
Vir Feb 19 10:53	Sco Mar 22 06:17	Cap Apr 23 11:46
Lib Feb 21 14:21	Sag Mar 24 15:42	Aqu Apr 26 00:40
Sco Feb 23 20:58	Cap Mar 27 03:50	Pis Apr 28 12:04
Sag Feb 26 07:09	Aqu Mar 29 16:33	Ari Apr 30 19:53
Cap Feb 28 19:44	Pis Apr 01 03:10	Tau May 02 23:52
Aqu Mar 02 08:13	Ari Apr 03 10:20	Gem May 05 01:22
Pis Mar 04 18:29	Tau Apr 05 14:27	Can May 07 02:13
Ari Mar 07 01:52	Gem Apr 07 16:57	Leo May 09 04:01
Tau Mar 09 07:00	Can Apr 09 19:15	Vir May 11 07:40
Gem Mar 11 10:44	Leo Apr 11 22:15	Lib May 13 13:27
Can Mar 13 13:50	Vir Apr 14 02:18	Sco May 15 21:16

Sag May 18 07:09	Aqu Jun 19 14:25	Ari Jul 21 19:08
Cap May 20 19:00	Pis Jun 22 02:50	Tau Jul 24 02:42
Aqu May 23 07:59	Ari Jun 24 12:53	Gem Jul 26 07:00
Pis May 25 20:06	Tau Jun 26 19:17	Can Jul 28 08:28
Ari May 28 05:06	Gem Jun 28 21:57	Leo Jul 30 08:23
Tau May 30 10:00	Can Jun 30 22:08	Vir Aug 01 08:27
Gem Jun 01 11:33	Leo Jul 02 21:37	Lib Aug 03 10:32
Can Jun 03 11:29	Vir Jul 04 22:19	Sco Aug 05 16:04
Leo Jun 05 11:45	Lib Jul 07 01:47	Sag Aug 08 01:30
Vir Jun 07 13:57	Sco Jul 09 08:48	Cap Aug 10 13:43
Lib Jun 09 18:58	Sag Jul 11 19:05	Aqu Aug 13 02:42
Sco Jun 12 02:55	Cap Jul 14 07:27	Pis Aug 15 14:40
Sag Jun 14 13:18	Aqu Jul 16 20:25	Ari Aug 18 00:42
Cap Jun 17 01:26	Pis Jul 19 08:42	Tau Aug 20 08:29

Gem Aug 22 13:53	Leo Sep 23 01:59	Lib Oct 24 14:29
Can Aug 24 16:58	Vir Sep 25 04:01	Sco Oct 26 19:23
Leo Aug 26 18:16	Lib Sep 27 06:21	Sag Oct 29 02:40
Vir Aug 28 18:54	Sco Sep 29 10:30	Cap Oct 31 13:01
Lib Aug 30 20:33	Sag Oct 01 17:49	Aqu Nov 03 01:39
Sco Sep 02 00:56	Cap Oct 04 04:42	Pis Nov 05 14:11
Sag Sep 04 09:08	Aqu Oct 06 17:32	Ari Nov 08 00:00
Cap Sep 06 20:46	Pis Oct 09 05:35	Tau Nov 10 06:11
Aqu Sep 09 09:43	Ari Oct 11 14:49	Gem Nov 12 09:26
Pis Sep 11 21:32	Tau Oct 13 21:04	Can Nov 14 11:20
Ari Sep 14 06:59	Gem Oct 16 01:17	Leo Nov 16 13:18
Tau Sep 16 14:04	Can Oct 18 04:36	Vir Nov 18 16:15
Gem Sep 18 19:21	Leo Oct 20 07:41	Lib Nov 20 20:34
Can Sep 20 23:14	Vir Oct 22 10:52	Sco Nov 23 02:32

Sag Nov 25 10:32	Aqu Dec 27 16:24	Aqu Jan 23 22:42
Cap Nov 27 20:56	Pis Dec 30 05:26	Pis Jan 26 11:37
Aqu Nov 30 09:25		Ari Jan 28 23:33
Pis Dec 02 22:21	**2001**	Tau Jan 31 09:19
Ari Dec 05 09:15	Ari Jan 01 17:13	Gem Feb 02 15:54
Tau Dec 07 16:25	Tau Jan 04 01:54	Can Feb 04 18:59
Gem Dec 09 19:49	Gem Jan 06 06:43	Leo Feb 06 19:20
Can Dec 11 20:47	Can Jan 08 08:07	Vir Feb 08 18:34
Leo Dec 13 21:08	Leo Jan 10 07:43	Lib Feb 10 18:45
Vir Dec 15 22:30	Vir Jan 12 07:25	Sco Feb 12 21:52
Lib Dec 18 02:01	Lib Jan 14 09:05	Sag Feb 15 05:02
Sco Dec 20 08:11	Sco Jan 16 14:03	Cap Feb 17 15:58
Sag Dec 22 16:56	Sag Jan 18 22:36	Aqu Feb 20 04:53
Cap Dec 25 03:53	Cap Jan 21 09:56	Pis Feb 22 17:44

Ari Feb 25 05:19	Gem Mar 29 04:00	Leo Apr 29 18:24
Tau Feb 27 15:04	Can Mar 31 09:21	Vir May 01 21:15
Gem Mar 01 22:34	Leo Apr 02 12:52	Lib May 03 23:49
Can Mar 04 03:23	Vir Apr 04 14:45	Sco May 06 03:00
Leo Mar 06 05:29	Lib Apr 06 15:56	Sag May 08 08:05
Vir Mar 08 05:43	Sco Apr 08 18:00	Cap May 10 16:09
Lib Mar 10 05:46	Sag Apr 10 22:47	Aqu May 13 03:19
Sco Mar 12 07:42	Cap Apr 13 07:20	Pis May 15 16:00
Sag Mar 14 13:17	Aqu Apr 15 19:10	Ari May 18 03:39
Cap Mar 16 23:02	Pis Apr 18 07:59	Tau May 20 12:27
Aqu Mar 19 11:35	Ari Apr 20 19:16	Gem May 22 18:11
Pis Mar 22 00:27	Tau Apr 23 03:54	Can May 24 21:41
Ari Mar 24 11:42	Gem Apr 25 10:10	Leo May 27 00:11
Tau Mar 26 20:49	Can Apr 27 14:48	Vir May 29 02:37

Lib May 31 05:40	Sag Jul 01 22:13	Aqu Aug 03 00:52
Sco Jun 02 09:56	Cap Jul 04 07:21	Pis Aug 05 13:29
Sag Jun 04 15:57	Aqu Jul 06 18:32	Ari Aug 08 02:03
Cap Jun 07 00:23	Pis Jul 09 07:04	Tau Aug 10 13:21
Aqu Jun 09 11:19	Ari Jul 11 19:34	Gem Aug 12 21:56
Pis Jun 11 23:52	Tau Jul 14 06:12	Can Aug 15 02:53
Ari Jun 14 12:01	Gem Jul 16 13:23	Leo Aug 17 04:24
Tau Jun 16 21:37	Can Jul 18 16:55	Vir Aug 19 03:52
Gem Jun 19 03:40	Leo Jul 20 17:42	Lib Aug 21 03:18
Can Jun 21 06:40	Vir Jul 22 17:28	Sco Aug 23 04:49
Leo Jun 23 07:54	Lib Jul 24 18:07	Sag Aug 25 09:59
Vir Jun 25 08:57	Sco Jul 26 21:17	Cap Aug 27 19:01
Lib Jun 27 11:10	Sag Jul 29 03:44	Aqu Aug 30 06:46
Sco Jun 29 15:28	Cap Jul 31 13:16	Pis Sep 01 19:31

Ari Sep 04 07:57	Gem Oct 06 10:10	Leo Nov 07 03:32
Tau Sep 06 19:16	Can Oct 08 17:18	Vir Nov 09 06:48
Gem Sep 09 04:39	Leo Oct 10 21:52	Lib Nov 11 08:52
Can Sep 11 11:07	Vir Oct 12 23:56	Sco Nov 13 10:44
Leo Sep 13 14:14	Lib Oct 15 00:25	Sag Nov 15 13:51
Vir Sep 15 14:38	Sco Oct 17 01:02	Cap Nov 17 19:39
Lib Sep 17 13:59	Sag Oct 19 03:47	Aqu Nov 20 04:54
Sco Sep 19 14:27	Cap Oct 21 10:12	Pis Nov 22 16:51
Sag Sep 21 18:01	Aqu Oct 23 20:26	Ari Nov 25 05:20
Cap Sep 24 01:48	Pis Oct 26 08:54	Tau Nov 27 16:04
Aqu Sep 26 13:04	Ari Oct 28 21:13	Gem Nov 30 00:02
Pis Sep 29 01:49	Tau Oct 31 07:46	Can Dec 02 05:29
Ari Oct 01 14:06	Gem Nov 02 16:11	Leo Dec 04 09:14
Tau Oct 04 00:59	Can Nov 04 22:42	Vir Dec 06 12:10

Lib Dec 08 14:56	Lib Jan 04 20:23	Sag Feb 05 10:21
Sco Dec 10 18:08	Sco Jan 06 23:41	Cap Feb 07 18:07
Sag Dec 12 22:29	Sag Jan 09 04:57	Aqu Feb 10 04:14
Cap Dec 15 04:47	Cap Jan 11 12:18	Pis Feb 12 15:52
Aqu Dec 17 13:43	Aqu Jan 13 21:41	Ari Feb 15 04:24
Pis Dec 20 01:09	Pis Jan 16 08:59	Tau Feb 17 16:57
Ari Dec 22 13:44	Ari Jan 18 21:34	Gem Feb 20 03:48
Tau Dec 25 01:10	Tau Jan 21 09:45	Can Feb 22 11:13
Gem Dec 27 09:37	Gem Jan 23 19:26	Leo Feb 24 14:34
Can Dec 29 14:38	Can Jan 26 01:15	Vir Feb 26 14:45
Leo Dec 31 17:08	Leo Jan 28 03:29	Lib Feb 28 13:46
	Vir Jan 30 03:39	Sco Mar 02 13:52
2002	Lib Feb 01 03:44	Sag Mar 04 16:54
	Sco Feb 03 05:34	Cap Mar 06 23:48
Vir Jan 02 18:33		

Aqu Mar 09 09:56	Ari Apr 10 16:39	Gem May 12 22:03
Pis Mar 11 21:56	Tau Apr 13 04:54	Can May 15 06:32
Ari Mar 14 10:33	Gem Apr 15 15:55	Leo May 17 12:50
Tau Mar 16 22:59	Can Apr 18 00:59	Vir May 19 16:59
Gem Mar 19 10:18	Leo Apr 20 07:19	Lib May 21 19:17
Can Mar 21 19:05	Vir Apr 22 10:33	Sco May 23 20:37
Leo Mar 24 00:10	Lib Apr 24 11:20	Sag May 25 22:19
Vir Mar 26 01:42	Sco Apr 26 11:15	Cap May 28 01:54
Lib Mar 28 01:03	Sag Apr 28 12:13	Aqu May 30 08:34
Sco Mar 30 00:21	Cap Apr 30 16:02	Pis Jun 01 18:36
Sag Apr 01 01:49	Aqu May 02 23:44	Ari Jun 04 06:50
Cap Apr 03 06:58	Pis May 05 10:45	Tau Jun 06 19:05
Aqu Apr 05 16:06	Ari May 07 23:21	Gem Jun 09 05:28
Pis Apr 08 03:57	Tau May 10 11:30	Can Jun 11 13:13

Leo Jun 13 18:38	Lib Jul 15 06:38	Sag Aug 15 18:24
Vir Jun 15 22:22	Sco Jul 17 09:12	Cap Aug 18 00:15
Lib Jun 18 01:10	Sag Jul 19 13:02	Aqu Aug 20 08:16
Sco Jun 20 03:41	Cap Jul 21 18:25	Pis Aug 22 18:10
Sag Jun 22 06:41	Aqu Jul 24 01:39	Ari Aug 25 05:46
Cap Jun 24 11:01	Pis Jul 26 11:04	Tau Aug 27 18:30
Aqu Jun 26 17:35	Ari Jul 28 22:38	Gem Aug 30 06:44
Pis Jun 29 03:00	Tau Jul 31 11:15	Can Sep 01 16:12
Ari Jul 01 14:48	Gem Aug 02 22:44	Leo Sep 03 21:34
Tau Jul 04 03:15	Can Aug 05 07:00	Vir Sep 05 23:14
Gem Jul 06 13:58	Leo Aug 07 11:25	Lib Sep 07 22:56
Can Jul 08 21:34	Vir Aug 09 13:02	Sco Sep 09 22:48
Leo Jul 11 02:06	Lib Aug 11 13:37	Sag Sep 12 00:44
Vir Jul 13 04:39	Sco Aug 13 15:00	Cap Sep 14 05:47

Aqu Sep 16 13:54	Ari Oct 18 18:12	Gem Nov 20 01:23
Pis Sep 19 00:17	Tau Oct 21 06:55	Can Nov 22 11:46
Ari Sep 21 12:10	Gem Oct 23 19:16	Leo Nov 24 19:58
Tau Sep 24 00:53	Can Oct 26 06:09	Vir Nov 27 01:40
Gem Sep 26 13:25	Leo Oct 28 14:18	Lib Nov 29 04:53
Can Sep 28 23:59	Vir Oct 30 18:58	Sco Dec 01 06:14
Leo Oct 01 06:57	Lib Nov 01 20:27	Sag Dec 03 06:57
Vir Oct 03 09:50	Sco Nov 03 20:09	Cap Dec 05 08:38
Lib Oct 05 09:50	Sag Nov 05 20:01	Aqu Dec 07 12:54
Sco Oct 07 08:57	Cap Nov 07 21:59	Pis Dec 09 20:46
Sag Oct 09 09:21	Aqu Nov 10 03:27	Ari Dec 12 07:57
Cap Oct 11 12:45	Pis Nov 12 12:41	Tau Dec 14 20:42
Aqu Oct 13 19:51	Ari Nov 15 00:37	Gem Dec 17 08:41
Pis Oct 16 06:06	Tau Nov 17 13:22	Can Dec 19 18:29

Leo Dec 22 01:47	Leo Jan 18 09:27	Lib Feb 18 23:47
Vir Dec 24 07:04	Vir Jan 20 13:30	Sco Feb 21 01:09
Lib Dec 26 10:52	Lib Jan 22 16:22	Sag Feb 23 03:45
Sco Dec 28 13:40	Sco Jan 24 19:08	Cap Feb 25 08:10
Sag Dec 30 16:00	Sag Jan 26 22:25	Aqu Feb 27 14:24
	Cap Jan 29 02:29	Pis Mar 01 22:25
2003	Aqu Jan 31 07:44	Ari Mar 04 08:29
Cap Jan 01 18:42	Pis Feb 02 14:54	Tau Mar 06 20:35
Aqu Jan 03 22:57	Ari Feb 05 00:44	Gem Mar 09 09:36
Pis Jan 06 05:56	Tau Feb 07 12:58	Can Mar 11 21:10
Ari Jan 08 16:14	Gem Feb 10 01:44	Leo Mar 14 05:05
Tau Jan 11 04:47	Can Feb 12 12:17	Vir Mar 16 08:51
Gem Jan 13 17:06	Leo Feb 14 19:03	Lib Mar 18 09:42
Can Jan 16 02:54	Vir Feb 16 22:21	Sco Mar 20 09:37

Sag Mar 22 10:33	Aqu Apr 23 01:58	Ari May 25 02:58
Cap Mar 24 13:48	Pis Apr 25 10:02	Tau May 27 15:31
Aqu Mar 26 19:50	Ari Apr 27 20:54	Gem May 30 04:30
Pis Mar 29 04:25	Tau Apr 30 09:25	Can Jun 01 16:26
Ari Mar 31 15:04	Gem May 02 22:26	Leo Jun 04 02:23
Tau Apr 03 03:19	Can May 05 10:40	Vir Jun 06 09:49
Gem Apr 05 16:23	Leo May 07 20:44	Lib Jun 08 14:28
Can Apr 08 04:35	Vir May 10 03:29	Sco Jun 10 16:37
Leo Apr 10 13:51	Lib May 12 06:41	Sag Jun 12 17:11
Vir Apr 12 19:05	Sco May 14 07:12	Cap Jun 14 17:37
Lib Apr 14 20:40	Sag May 16 06:42	Aqu Jun 16 19:41
Sco Apr 16 20:15	Cap May 18 07:03	Pis Jun 19 00:57
Sag Apr 18 19:51	Aqu May 20 10:01	Ari Jun 21 10:05
Cap Apr 20 21:20	Pis May 22 16:40	Tau Jun 23 22:14

Gem Jun 26 11:11	Leo Jul 28 15:15	Lib Aug 29 08:40
Can Jun 28 22:50	Vir Jul 30 21:25	Sco Aug 31 10:59
Leo Jul 01 08:12	Lib Aug 02 01:46	Sag Sep 02 13:31
Vir Jul 03 15:14	Sco Aug 04 05:11	Cap Sep 04 16:50
Lib Jul 05 20:19	Sag Aug 06 08:10	Aqu Sep 06 21:14
Sco Jul 07 23:42	Cap Aug 08 11:02	Pis Sep 09 03:06
Sag Jul 10 01:47	Aqu Aug 10 14:23	Ari Sep 11 11:09
Cap Jul 12 03:20	Pis Aug 12 19:18	Tau Sep 13 21:49
Aqu Jul 14 05:37	Ari Aug 15 03:00	Gem Sep 16 10:31
Pis Jul 16 10:14	Tau Aug 17 13:52	Can Sep 18 23:06
Ari Jul 18 18:18	Gem Aug 20 02:40	Leo Sep 21 09:01
Tau Jul 21 05:47	Can Aug 22 14:43	Vir Sep 23 15:02
Gem Jul 23 18:41	Leo Aug 24 23:46	Lib Sep 25 17:48
Can Jul 26 06:22	Vir Aug 27 05:25	Sco Sep 27 18:51

Sag Sep 29 19:56	Aqu Oct 31 08:41	Ari Dec 02 05:55
Cap Oct 01 22:21	Pis Nov 02 14:52	Tau Dec 04 17:29
Aqu Oct 04 02:45	Ari Nov 05 00:02	Gem Dec 07 06:25
Pis Oct 06 09:20	Tau Nov 07 11:28	Can Dec 09 19:10
Ari Oct 08 18:07	Gem Nov 10 00:13	Leo Dec 12 06:39
Tau Oct 11 05:04	Can Nov 12 13:09	Vir Dec 14 16:05
Gem Oct 13 17:44	Leo Nov 15 00:46	Lib Dec 16 22:44
Can Oct 16 06:40	Vir Nov 17 09:34	Sco Dec 19 02:18
Leo Oct 18 17:40	Lib Nov 19 14:40	Sag Dec 21 03:14
Vir Oct 21 00:59	Sco Nov 21 16:22	Cap Dec 23 02:55
Lib Oct 23 04:25	Sag Nov 23 16:02	Aqu Dec 25 03:13
Sco Oct 25 05:07	Cap Nov 25 15:31	Pis Dec 27 06:09
Sag Oct 27 04:54	Aqu Nov 27 16:48	Ari Dec 29 13:09
Cap Oct 29 05:36	Pis Nov 29 21:26	

2004

Tau Jan 01 00:01	Gem Jan 30 20:17	Leo Mar 03 04:16
Gem Jan 03 12:57	Can Feb 02 09:02	Vir Mar 05 12:16
Can Jan 06 01:37	Leo Feb 04 19:49	Lib Mar 07 17:30
Leo Jan 08 12:37	Vir Feb 07 04:01	Sco Mar 09 21:02
Vir Jan 10 21:36	Lib Feb 09 10:11	Sag Mar 11 23:56
Lib Jan 13 04:37	Sco Feb 11 14:56	Cap Mar 14 02:51
Sco Jan 15 09:31	Sag Feb 13 18:34	Aqu Mar 16 06:09
Sag Jan 17 12:16	Cap Feb 15 21:13	Pis Mar 18 10:26
Cap Jan 19 13:23	Aqu Feb 17 23:27	Ari Mar 20 16:28
Aqu Jan 21 14:10	Pis Feb 20 02:27	Tau Mar 23 01:09
Pis Jan 23 16:28	Ari Feb 22 07:45	Gem Mar 25 12:34
Ari Jan 25 22:06	Tau Feb 24 16:30	Can Mar 28 01:22
Tau Jan 28 07:46	Gem Feb 27 04:22	Leo Mar 30 13:05
	Can Feb 29 17:11	Vir Apr 01 21:43

Lib Apr 04 02:50	Sag May 05 16:07	Aqu Jun 06 02:10
Sco Apr 06 05:23	Cap May 07 16:16	Pis Jun 08 04:38
Sag Apr 08 06:49	Aqu May 09 17:45	Ari Jun 10 10:50
Cap Apr 10 08:33	Pis May 11 21:52	Tau Jun 12 20:36
Aqu Apr 12 11:33	Ari May 14 05:02	Gem Jun 15 08:43
Pis Apr 14 16:23	Tau May 16 14:56	Can Jun 17 21:36
Ari Apr 16 23:24	Gem May 19 02:46	Leo Jun 20 10:03
Tau Apr 19 08:42	Can May 21 15:34	Vir Jun 22 21:08
Gem Apr 21 20:09	Leo May 24 04:06	Lib Jun 25 05:49
Can Apr 24 08:55	Vir May 26 14:50	Sco Jun 27 11:10
Leo Apr 26 21:13	Lib May 28 22:20	Sag Jun 29 13:14
Vir Apr 29 06:59	Sco May 31 02:06	Cap Jul 01 13:00
Lib May 01 13:00	Sag Jun 02 02:51	Aqu Jul 03 12:22
Sco May 03 15:37	Cap Jun 04 02:12	Pis Jul 05 13:27

Ari Jul 07 18:02	Gem Aug 08 21:32	Leo Sep 10 06:05
Tau Jul 10 02:50	Can Aug 11 10:19	Vir Sep 12 16:15
Gem Jul 12 14:44	Leo Aug 13 22:28	Lib Sep 14 23:52
Can Jul 15 03:40	Vir Aug 16 08:48	Sco Sep 17 05:24
Leo Jul 17 15:55	Lib Aug 18 17:08	Sag Sep 19 09:28
Vir Jul 20 02:43	Sco Aug 20 23:35	Cap Sep 21 12:34
Lib Jul 22 11:37	Sag Aug 23 04:07	Aqu Sep 23 15:09
Sco Jul 24 18:07	Cap Aug 25 06:46	Pis Sep 25 17:55
Sag Jul 26 21:46	Aqu Aug 27 08:07	Ari Sep 27 21:57
Cap Jul 28 22:56	Pis Aug 29 09:33	Tau Sep 30 04:23
Aqu Jul 30 22:54	Ari Aug 31 12:46	Gem Oct 02 13:55
Pis Aug 01 23:35	Tau Sep 02 19:15	Can Oct 05 01:53
Ari Aug 04 03:00	Gem Sep 05 05:24	Leo Oct 07 14:22
Tau Aug 06 10:26	Can Sep 07 17:49	Vir Oct 10 00:58

Lib Oct 12 08:30	Sag Nov 13 00:55	Aqu Dec 14 11:10
Sco Oct 14 13:09	Cap Nov 15 01:32	Pis Dec 16 12:24
Sag Oct 16 15:57	Aqu Nov 17 02:39	Ari Dec 18 16:52
Cap Oct 18 18:06	Pis Nov 19 05:37	Tau Dec 21 00:52
Aqu Oct 20 20:37	Ari Nov 21 11:11	Gem Dec 23 11:32
Pis Oct 23 00:13	Tau Nov 23 19:15	Can Dec 25 23:37
Ari Oct 25 05:24	Gem Nov 26 05:24	Leo Dec 28 12:13
Tau Oct 27 12:37	Can Nov 28 17:10	Vir Dec 31 00:32
Gem Oct 29 22:11	Leo Dec 01 05:49	
Can Nov 01 09:52	Vir Dec 03 17:59	**2005**
Leo Nov 03 22:31	Lib Dec 06 03:45	Lib Jan 02 11:18
Vir Nov 06 09:58	Sco Dec 08 09:41	Sco Jan 04 18:58
Lib Nov 08 18:22	Sag Dec 10 11:52	Sag Jan 06 22:42
Sco Nov 10 23:03	Cap Dec 12 11:41	Cap Jan 08 23:09

Aqu Jan 10 22:07	Ari Feb 11 10:22	Gem Mar 15 08:44
Pis Jan 12 21:51	Tau Feb 13 15:18	Can Mar 17 19:43
Ari Jan 15 00:27	Gem Feb 16 00:18	Leo Mar 20 08:16
Tau Jan 17 07:06	Can Feb 18 12:12	Vir Mar 22 20:09
Gem Jan 19 17:23	Leo Feb 21 00:53	Lib Mar 25 05:59
Can Jan 22 05:41	Vir Feb 23 12:43	Sco Mar 27 13:27
Leo Jan 24 18:20	Lib Feb 25 22:57	Sag Mar 29 18:55
Vir Jan 27 06:23	Sco Feb 28 07:19	Cap Mar 31 22:47
Lib Jan 29 17:12	Sag Mar 02 13:28	Aqu Apr 03 01:30
Sco Feb 01 01:49	Cap Mar 04 17:11	Pis Apr 05 03:45
Sag Feb 03 07:20	Aqu Mar 06 18:48	Ari Apr 07 06:27
Cap Feb 05 09:30	Pis Mar 08 19:32	Tau Apr 09 10:50
Aqu Feb 07 09:25	Ari Mar 10 21:03	Gem Apr 11 17:54
Pis Feb 09 08:59	Tau Mar 13 01:06	Can Apr 14 04:03

Leo Apr 16 16:16	Lib May 18 23:28	Sag Jun 19 20:43
Vir Apr 19 04:26	Sco May 21 06:47	Cap Jun 21 21:51
Lib Apr 21 14:25	Sag May 23 10:36	Aqu Jun 23 21:36
Sco Apr 23 21:24	Cap May 25 12:10	Pis Jun 25 22:03
Sag Apr 26 01:44	Aqu May 27 13:09	Ari Jun 28 00:52
Cap Apr 28 04:32	Pis May 29 15:09	Tau Jun 30 06:44
Aqu Apr 30 06:53	Ari May 31 19:07	Gem Jul 02 15:25
Pis May 02 09:42	Tau Jun 03 01:19	Can Jul 05 02:07
Ari May 04 13:36	Gem Jun 05 09:35	Leo Jul 07 14:10
Tau May 06 19:01	Can Jun 07 19:46	Vir Jul 10 02:56
Gem May 09 02:28	Leo Jun 10 07:39	Lib Jul 12 15:08
Can May 11 12:20	Vir Jun 12 20:21	Sco Jul 15 00:49
Leo May 14 00:16	Lib Jun 15 07:57	Sag Jul 17 06:34
Vir May 16 12:45	Sco Jun 17 16:22	Cap Jul 19 08:25

Aqu Jul 21 07:54	Ari Aug 21 18:00	Gem Sep 22 12:07
Pis Jul 23 07:11	Tau Aug 23 20:58	Can Sep 24 21:10
Ari Jul 25 08:23	Gem Aug 26 03:43	Leo Sep 27 09:02
Tau Jul 27 12:55	Can Aug 28 13:57	Vir Sep 29 21:43
Gem Jul 29 21:02	Leo Aug 31 02:14	Lib Oct 02 09:23
Can Aug 01 07:52	Vir Sep 02 14:55	Sco Oct 04 19:02
Leo Aug 03 20:09	Lib Sep 05 02:51	Sag Oct 07 02:27
Vir Aug 06 08:53	Sco Sep 07 13:09	Cap Oct 09 07:42
Lib Aug 08 21:07	Sag Sep 09 21:01	Aqu Oct 11 11:04
Sco Aug 11 07:33	Cap Sep 12 01:55	Pis Oct 13 13:04
Sag Aug 13 14:45	Aqu Sep 14 04:01	Ari Oct 15 14:39
Cap Aug 15 18:12	Pis Sep 16 04:24	Tau Oct 17 17:04
Aqu Aug 17 18:38	Ari Sep 18 04:42	Gem Oct 19 21:44
Pis Aug 19 17:52	Tau Sep 20 06:47	Can Oct 22 05:40

Leo Oct 24 16:48	Lib Nov 26 01:56	Sag Dec 28 03:42
Vir Oct 27 05:27	Sco Nov 28 11:31	Cap Dec 30 06:34
Lib Oct 29 17:14	Sag Nov 30 17:31	
Sco Nov 01 02:27	Cap Dec 02 20:41	
Sag Nov 03 08:54	Aqu Dec 04 22:36	
Cap Nov 05 13:16	Pis Dec 07 00:44	
Aqu Nov 07 16:30	Ari Dec 09 04:02	
Pis Nov 09 19:22	Tau Dec 11 08:46	
Ari Nov 11 22:22	Gem Dec 13 14:59	
Tau Nov 14 02:02	Can Dec 15 23:01	
Gem Nov 16 07:09	Leo Dec 18 09:18	
Can Nov 18 14:42	Vir Dec 20 21:38	
Leo Nov 21 01:10	Lib Dec 23 10:25	
Vir Nov 23 13:41	Sco Dec 25 21:02